CHILDREN'S
ENCYCLOPEDIA
OF OCEAN LIFE

Claudia Martin

ARCTURUS

Picture Credits:
Key: b–bottom, t–top, c–center, l–left, r–right

Alamy Stock Photo: 1, 76–77 (Michael Siluk), 8–9 (Scenics and Science), 10–11 (Andrey Nekrasov), 13t, 26–27, 45t (Paulo Oliveira), 14–15, 60–61 (Helmut Corneli), 20–21 (Solvin Zankl/Nature Picture Library), 23t, 106b (SeaTops), 24t (PF–(usna1)), 26c (NC Collections), 28–29 (blickwinkel), 30–31 (Chris Gomersall), 34–35, 62–63, 84c (David Fleetham), 38–39 (Georgette Apol/Steve Bloom Images), 42c (Norbert Wu/Minden Pictures), 42–43 (Solvin Zankl), 44–45 (World History Archive), 66b (Antonio Busiello/Robert Harding), 68–69 (Reinhard Dirscherl), 73t (Arco Images GmbH/G. Lacz), 82b (cbimages), 84b (WaterFrame), 86–87 (Masa Ushioda/Stephen Frink Collection), 88–89 (Tony Wu/Nature Picture Library), 92t (Pete Ryan/National Geographic Image Collection), 100b (blickwinkel/Frischknecht), 110–111 (Paul R. Sterry/Nature Photographers Ltd), 114c (FLPA), 114–115 (Richard Mittleman/Gon2Foto), 116b (David Tipling Photo Library), 118–119 (Rodrigo Friscione/Cultura Creative (RF)), 123b (Doug Allan/Nature Picture Library); **FLPA Images:** 16c (Mike Parry/Minden Pictures), 18b, 86b, 109c (Tui De Roy/Minden Pictures), 32l, 42b, 74c (Photo Researchers), 40–41, 90–91 (Flip Nicklin/Minden Pictures), 43t, 70–71 (Norbert Wu/Minden Pictures), 54c (Scott Leslie/Minden Pictures), 68c (Bruce Rasner, Jeffrey Rotman/Biosphoto), 72b (Steve Trewhella), 74–75 (Norbert Probst/Imagebroker), 92c (Hiroya Minakuchi/Minden Pictures), 92–93 (Peter Verhoog/Minden Pictures), 98c (Suzi Eszterhas/Minden Pictures), 98–99 (Frans Lanting), 99b (Kevin Schafer/Minden Pictures), 104–105 (Christophe Migeon/Biosphoto), 110c (Glenn Bartley, BIA/Minden Pictures), 120c (Jack Perks); **Getty Images:** 22–23 (Daniela Dirscherl), 54b (Mark Conlin), 58–59 (ullstein bild), 78–79 (viridis), 82–83 (marrio31), 84–85 (Rodrigo Friscione), 106–107 (Georgette Douwma), 112–113 (D Williams Photography); **Science Photo Library:** 7t (Gary Hincks); **Shutterstock:** 4c (Marut Syannikroth), 4b (AshtonEa), 4–5, 76bc, 76br (Cigdem Sean Cooper), 5t, 50b (SergeUWPhoto), 5b (Ian Dyball), 6c (Tea Oor), 6br (R McIntyre), 6–7 (titoOnz), 8cl (Dr. Norbert Lange), 8cc (Agami Photo Agency), 8cr (Craig Milson), 8bl (Gerald Robert Fischer), 8bc (Rattiya Phongdumhyu), 8br (Dmitry Reznichenko), 9tl (John A Anderson), 9tr (Ocean Image Photography), 10cr (CK Ma), 10cl (Oksana Maksymova), 10b (painapple), 11t (feathercollector), 12cr (Anna Filippenok), 12bl (Gena Melendrez), 12bc (Shane Gross), 12br (Joe Quinn), 12–13 (aquapix), 14cr (Grobler du Preez), 14bl (Joanne Weston), 14bc (Jeff Stamer), 14br, 47b, 48–49 (zaferkizilkaya), 15b (Chase Dekker), 16b (Tomas Kotouc), 16–17 (Jack Pokoj), 17b (Stephanie Rousseau), 18c (Collins93), 18–19 (Andrew Astbury), 19b (Roger Clark ARPS), 20c, 26b (NoPainNoGain), 20b, 87t, 89b (wildestanimal), 21b, 102c, 104b (Tarpan), 22c (Ethan Daniels), 22b, 36b, 38b (Rich Carey), 24c, 77t (Dennis Jacobsen), 24b (Zaruba Ondrej), 24–25 (Gabriel Guzman), 25b (LouisLotterPhotography), 27t (Aleksander Karpenko), 28c (Paul A Carpenter), 28b (Bildagentur Zoonar GmbH), 29t (Gerald Marella), 30cl (Nigel Wallace), 30cr (FredChan), 30b (Cary Kalscheuer), 31tr (pzAxe), 32b (aDam Wildlife), 32–33, 58b, 63t (Damsea), 33b (wonderisland), 34c (Gilberto Villasana), 34b (steve estvanik), 35b (NatureDiver), 36c, 37t, 70b, 94c (Laura Dinraths), 36–37 (David John Ciavarella), 39c (fenkieandreas), 39b (Vladimir Wrangel), 40c (reisegraf.ch), 41t (Rudmer Zwerver), 46c, 60c (Richard Whitcombe), 46–47, 64c, 65b (blue-sea.cz), 48c (Martin Prochazkacz), 48b (Kondratuk Aleksei), 49b (Tignogartnahc), 50c (subphoto), 50–51 (Yusran Abdul Rahman), 51t (Evan Hallein), 52c (Jay Gao), 52b (Petr Malyshev), 52–53 (Uwe Bergwitz), 53t (Jarib), 54–55 (Levent Konuk), 55t (RLS Photo), 56c (AlessandroZocc), 56b (Vladyslav Danilin), 56–57 (Bill45), 57t (Arunee Rodloy), 58c, 114b (Brian Lasenby), 59b (Joe Belanger), 60b (Eugene Kalenkovich), 61t, 69b (Mark Willian Kirkland), 62c, 81t, 83t (orlandin), 62b, 124–125 (Brandon B), 64b (Leo Lorenzo), 64–65 (Levent Albas), 66c (Sergey Uryadnikov), 66–67 (Alex Rush), 67t (makeitahabit), 68b, 70c, 88c, 91b (Andrea Izzotti), 71b (Roman Vintonyak), 72c (Tropical studio), 72–73 (scubaluna), 74b (Gerald Robert Fischer), 75c (Michael Warwick), 76c (Alex_Vinci), 78c (divedog), 78b (Silk-stocking), 79b (ligio), 80c (yaodiving), 80bc (Kichigin), 80br (NaniP), 80–81 (besjunior), 82c (Anne Frijling), 85b (lunamarina), 86c (Jo Crebbin), 88b (John Wollwerth), 90c (Tory Kallman), 90b (Andrew Sutton), 94b (Liquid Productions, LLC), 94–95 (Greg Amptman), 95b (Jiri Prochazka), 96c (AndreAnita), 96b (Alexey Seafarer), 96–97 (FloridaStock), 97b (Caleb Foster), 98b (Chanonry), 100c (Ondrej Prosicky), 100–101 (Hal Brindley), 101b (Pascal Halder), 102b, 116c (David Osborn), 102–103 (Pat Stornebrink), 103b (Nicram Sabod), 104c (Wonderly Imaging), 105c (Philip Bird LRPS CPAGB), 106c (shakeelmsm), 107t (William Healy Photography), 108c (Ery Azmeer), 108b (Elements_Brisbane), 108–109, 119b (Don Mammoser), 110b (anirbandas08081986), 111c (John L. Absher), 112b (Bernie Van Der Vyver), 113tc (Karel Gallas), 113tr (Wolf Avni), 113b (Dennis Von Linden), 115b (Frank Fichtmueller), 116–117 (Jeremy Richards), 117t (jaroslava V), 118c (Ray Hennessy), 118b (RHIMAGE), 120bc (Erni), 120br (Brian E Kushner), 120–121 (Simonas Minkevicius), 121b (Rob Francis), 122c, 122b (Nick Pecker), 122–123 (Enrique Aguirre), 124c (ChameleonsEye), 124b (MZPHOTO.CZ), 125b (Lynsey Allan); **Wikimedia Commons:** 40b (Uwe Kils), 44t (MARUM – Zentrum für Marine Umweltwissenschaften, Universität Bremen), 44b (NOAA Okeanos Explorer Program, Galapagos Rift Expedition 2011), 46b (Aquapix and Expedition to the Deep Slope 2007, NOAA-OE), 92b (Paula Olson, NOAA), 93t (GregTheBusker). All cover images are from Shutterstock.

ARCTURUS

This edition published in 2021 by Arcturus Publishing Limited
26/27 Bickels Yard, 151–153 Bermondsey Street,
London SE1 3HA

Consultant: Jules Howard
Author and Editor: Claudia Martin
Designer: Amy McSimpson

ISBN: 978-1-78950-601-3
CH007200US
Supplier 29, Date 0821, Print run 11609

Printed in China

In this book, one billion means one thousand million (1,000,000,000) and one trillion means one million million (1,000,000,000,000).

CHILDREN'S ENCYCLOPEDIA OF OCEAN LIFE

CONTENTS

Watery World

The oceans are so wide and deep that they provide 90 percent of all the living space on Earth. Their water offers food, transport, shelter—and life—to trillions of living things, from lobsters that scuttle across the seafloor to gulls that soar high above the waves.

Many Habitats

From wave-washed beaches to the dark ocean floor, from coral reefs to polar ice, there are many different ocean habitats. Some habitats offer shelter for animals, such as soft sand for tunneling or seagrass for hiding. Every habitat offers food for its inhabitants, whether that is sardines to snap up or seaweed to graze on.

The rusty parrotfish lives on coral reefs in the Indian Ocean.

Its mouth, shaped like a parrot's beak, has many sharp teeth for scraping algae off coral.

This mangrove crab hides from predators by burrowing into wet mud along the shore. It surfaces to hunt for plants and small animals to eat.

Different Bodies

The bodies of ocean animals are well suited to their habitat. Many deep-sea fish have large eyes for seeing in dim waters, while penguins have a thick layer of fat for warmth in freezing seas. Studying each animal's body can also reveal its method of travel—or that it does not travel at all. Dolphins have a sleek body for swimming fast in the open ocean. Tube worms root themselves to the ocean floor, pulling inside their tough tube for safety.

Sea spiders are not closely related to land spiders, although they walk in a similar way on their eight legs. They can also swim over the seafloor by waving their legs.

Amazing Life Cycles

When it is time to reproduce, most fish release many jelly-like eggs into the water and then swim away. Seabirds lay just one or two tough-shelled eggs on land and care for their chicks until they are old enough to hunt. Porpoises give birth to live young, called calves, while some comb jellies can clone themselves by splitting off parts of their own body.

Unlike most fish, the male jawfish takes care of his eggs by holding them in his mouth.

This parrotfish started life as a brown-colored female, before changing both sex and appearance to become a bright-colored male.

Together and Apart

Great white sharks usually hunt alone, while surgeonfish swim in groups called shoals for protection. Whales live in groups called pods, whistling, clicking, and singing to each other. Although seabirds often nest in noisy colonies, albatrosses spend the rest of the year flying alone, watching for fish in the water below. Corals live in groups called colonies, made of thousands of joined, identical coral polyps.

Playing is quite unusual for ocean animals, but seals and other mammals are among the creatures that like to have fun together.

The Five Oceans

Water covers more than two-thirds of our planet's surface. Nearly 97 percent of this water is saltwater, with just 3 percent made up of freshwater in rivers, ponds, and lakes. Saltwater fills a vast world ocean, which humans have named as five oceans.

Salty Water

The ocean tastes salty because it contains particles of sodium and chloride. Together, these make sodium chloride, which is better known as table salt. These particles, and other minerals, arrived in the ocean through a process called weathering. As rain falls, it collects carbon dioxide from the air. This gas mixes with the water to make carbonic acid. Acids can wear away materials, so as rainwater runs over rocks, it carries away tiny particles, including sodium and chloride. Rivers and streams carry the particles to the ocean.

The **Pacific Ocean** is both the largest and deepest ocean, with an average depth of 13,000 ft (4,000 m).

The **Arctic Ocean** is almost completely covered by ice in winter.

In Pattani, Thailand, salt is gathered on the beach. When the seawater evaporates, or turns to gas, in the hot sun, it leaves behind the solid salt.

Islands of the Maldives, in the Indian Ocean

AREAS OF THE OCEANS

Pacific Ocean: 65,144,000 sq miles (168,723,000 sq km)

Atlantic Ocean: 32,870,000 sq miles (85,133,000 sq km)

Indian Ocean: 27,243,000 sq miles (70,560,000 sq km)

Southern Ocean: 8,479,000 sq miles (21,960,000 sq km)

Arctic Ocean: 6,007,000 sq miles (15,558,000 sq km)

DID YOU KNOW? If all the salt in the ocean was spread across Earth's land, it would form a layer more than 500 ft (150 m) thick.

Moving Water

Ocean water is constantly moving. As the wind blows across the surface, it whips up waves, which travel right across the ocean until they curl over and "break" on the shore. Currents are great rivers of water that snake around the oceans. Some currents are caused by wind, while others are caused by differences in water temperature. At the surface or closer to the equator, the water is warmer. Warm water rises, while cold water sinks, setting off global movements.

Major currents flow clockwise in the northern hemisphere and counterclockwise in the southern hemisphere. These directions are caused by the turning of the planet, which shifts water and winds to the right north of the equator, but the opposite way south of the equator.

The temperature at the surface of the **Atlantic Ocean** ranges from over 86°F (30°C) at the equator to 28°F (–2°C).

The **Indian Ocean** is the warmest ocean, with surface temperatures always higher than 71°F (22°C).

The **Southern Ocean** surrounds the continent of Antarctica.

7

A Wealth of Life

Around 4 billion years ago, the first living things formed in the oceans. They were microorganisms, too small to be seen by the human eye. Today, microorganisms make up 70 percent of the weight of all the ocean's living things. Larger life forms include animals, plants, and fungi.

Kingdoms

Scientists often divide living things into "kingdoms," based on characteristics such as the number and type of cells from which they are made. Cells are the building blocks for all living things. All the kingdoms include "marine" forms, which live in or around the ocean.

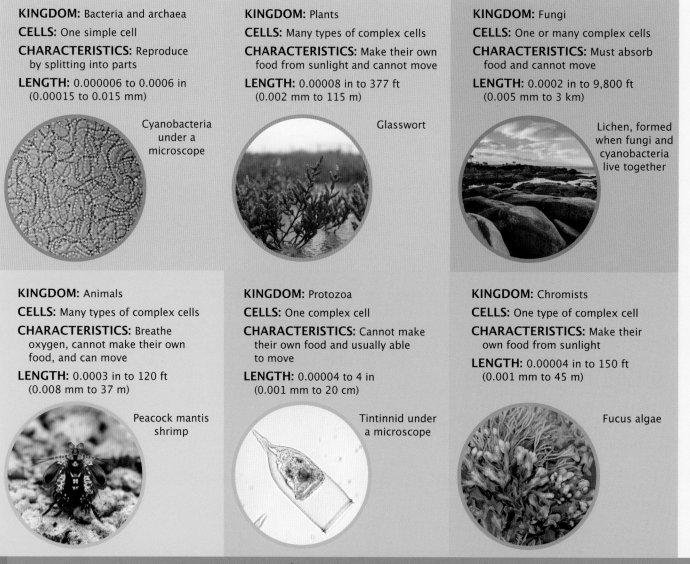

KINGDOM: Bacteria and archaea

CELLS: One simple cell

CHARACTERISTICS: Reproduce by splitting into parts

LENGTH: 0.000006 to 0.0006 in (0.00015 to 0.015 mm)

Cyanobacteria under a microscope

KINGDOM: Plants

CELLS: Many types of complex cells

CHARACTERISTICS: Make their own food from sunlight and cannot move

LENGTH: 0.00008 in to 377 ft (0.002 mm to 115 m)

Glasswort

KINGDOM: Fungi

CELLS: One or many complex cells

CHARACTERISTICS: Must absorb food and cannot move

LENGTH: 0.0002 in to 9,800 ft (0.005 mm to 3 km)

Lichen, formed when fungi and cyanobacteria live together

KINGDOM: Animals

CELLS: Many types of complex cells

CHARACTERISTICS: Breathe oxygen, cannot make their own food, and can move

LENGTH: 0.0003 in to 120 ft (0.008 mm to 37 m)

Peacock mantis shrimp

KINGDOM: Protozoa

CELLS: One complex cell

CHARACTERISTICS: Cannot make their own food and usually able to move

LENGTH: 0.00004 to 4 in (0.001 mm to 20 cm)

Tintinnid under a microscope

KINGDOM: Chromists

CELLS: One type of complex cell

CHARACTERISTICS: Make their own food from sunlight

LENGTH: 0.00004 in to 150 ft (0.001 mm to 45 m)

Fucus algae

DID YOU KNOW? Around 250,000 marine species have been named, but scientists think there are at least 750,000 more to be found.

Species

A species, such as the great hammerhead shark, is a group of living things that can mate with one another and produce healthy babies. Scientists arrange species into bigger groups, such as genus, order, class, and kingdom, based on their similarities. The great hammerhead is in the genus of hammerhead sharks, in the order of ground sharks, in the class of cartilaginous fish, in the kingdom of animals.

This stove-pipe sponge and the yellow tube sponge (above right) are two species of sponges in the class of demosponges in the animal kingdom.

Diatoms may be round, rods, or star shapes.

Diatoms are chromists that float through the oceans, turning sunlight into energy.

No more than 0.008 in (0.2 mm) long, a diatom is a single cell, surrounded by a glass-like wall. These diatoms are seen under a microscope.

Marine Invertebrates

With its squidgy, jelly-like body, the warty comb jelly is in the ctenophore phylum.

Around 580 to 550 million years ago, the first animals moved in the oceans. These early animals were all invertebrates. Invertebrates are animals that do not have a backbone—or any other bones inside their body. Apart from that, invertebrates can be very different from each other.

Many Different Bodies

Scientists divide invertebrates into 30 different groups, called phylums, based on their body plan. In contrast, all animals with a backbone—fish, mammals, reptiles, amphibians, and birds—are in just one phylum. Some invertebrates, such as nematode worms, are completely soft-bodied. Others, called arthropods, have an exoskeleton, or hard covering, to protect their boneless body. Marine arthropods include crabs and lobsters. Other invertebrates, called mollusks, have a muscly covering called a mantle. In some mollusks, such as snails and clams, the mantle builds a hard shell.

Members of the chordate phylum, sea squirts are tube-shaped animals that attach to rocks. They feed by sucking in water and tiny creatures.

The tiger egg cowry is a species of sea snail in the mollusk phylum.

Looking at Fossils

Fossils are the preserved remains of ancient living things. Scientists study fossils to find out how animals have evolved, or changed over time, and when different groups of animals first appeared. The oldest invertebrate fossils are of simple sponges.

This is fossilized brain coral, which is in the cnidarian phylum.

MARINE INVERTEBRATE RECORDS

Heaviest: Colossal squid, up to 1,650 lb (750 kg) and 46 ft (14 m) long

Longest: Lion's mane jellyfish, up to 120 ft (37 m)

Shortest: Myxozoa, which live in or on other animals, as small as 0.0003 in (0.008 mm)

Fastest swimmer: Flying squid, up to 25 mph (40 km/h)

Longest living: Glass sponges, possibly up to 15,000 years

Neon flying squid

It swims, very slowly, by waving the combs that run in strips down its body. The strips glow when the comb jelly is disturbed.

The warty comb jelly is just 2.8 to 4.7 in (7 to 12 cm) long.

DID YOU KNOW? Invertebrates make up 96 percent of all the species of animals living in and around the world's oceans.

Marine Fish

At least 16,000 species of fish live in the ocean. Fish breathe by taking oxygen from the water using their gills. Most fish swim by waving their body or tail, while steering with their fins. Many fish, but not all of them, have skin covered in hard plates called scales.

Breathing through Gills

Fish breathe by gulping water into their mouth. Water contains lots of oxygen. The water flows through the gills, which are filled with tiny blood vessels. The blood vessels soak up the oxygen, which the fish's heart pumps round the body. The used water is released through the gill slits.

Fish Features

KEY

1. GILLS
2. HEART
3. PELVIC FIN
4. STOMACH
5. ANAL FIN
6. CAUDAL FIN
7. DORSAL FINS

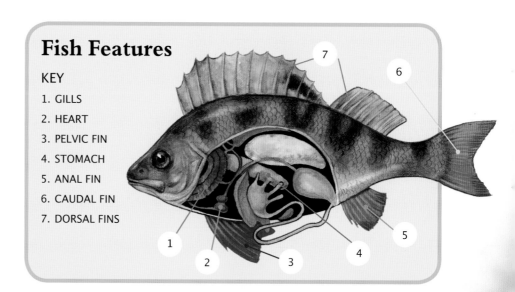

Classes of Fish

There are three classes of fish, which have different body features. The earliest fish to evolve were jawless fish, but most of them are now extinct.

JAWLESS FISH

CHARACTERISTICS:
These fish have no jaws for biting, so they feed by sucking. They have long, scale-less bodies.

SPECIES: Hagfish and lampreys

A lamprey mouth

CARTILAGINOUS FISH

CHARACTERISTICS:
This class of jawed fish have a skeleton made of bendy cartilage. Their skin has many tooth-like scales.

SPECIES: Sharks, skates, and rays

Thresher shark

BONY FISH

CHARACTERISTICS:
These jawed fish have skeletons made of bone. Their scales are usually smooth and overlapping.

SPECIES: All other fish

Yellowtail snapper

Heaviest and longest: Whale shark, up to 47,000 lb (21,300 kg) and 41.5 ft (12.65 m) long

Longest bony fish: Giant oarfish, up to 36 ft (11 m)

Shortest: Male *Photocorynus spiniceps* anglerfish, as small as 0.24 in (6.2 mm)

Fastest swimmer: Black marlin, up to 65 mph (105 km/h)

Longest living: Greenland shark, possibly up to 400 years

Giant oarfish

Like in other bony fish, the gill slit is protected by a hard cover called the operculum.

The squirrelfish is nocturnal, or active at night. It has large eyes so it can gather as much light as possible.

Pectoral fins, on either side of the head, help with steering.

DID YOU KNOW? Female sunfish produce more eggs than any other fish, releasing up to 300 million of them into the water.

Marine Mammals

Around 126 species of mammals spend all or part of their life in the ocean. Like other mammals—including humans—these animals need to breathe air, so they come to the water surface regularly. All female mammals feed their young on milk.

Family Life

All marine mammals give birth to live young. Apart from polar bears, which have up to three cubs, marine mammals have just one baby at a time, which they look after for several months or even years. All marine mammals make sounds to communicate with each other, from the songs of whales to the barks of seals.

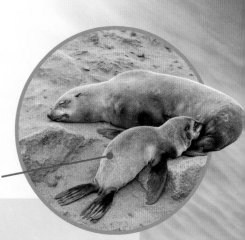

A Cape fur seal feeds her pup on milk for the first six months.

Groups of Marine Mammals

Marine mammals are not all closely related to each other: They belong to different scientific groups with quite different bodies and lifestyles.

CETACEANS

CHARACTERISTICS:
These mammals never leave the water. They have a streamlined body and two limbs that are flippers.

SPECIES: Around 85 whales, dolphins, and porpoises

Minke whale

SEA COWS

CHARACTERISTICS:
Sea cows never leave the water. They have a rounded body and two limbs that are flippers

SPECIES: 3 manatees and a dugong

West Indian manatee

CARNIVORANS

CHARACTERISTICS:
These clawed meat-eaters spend part of their life on land. They have four limbs, which are flipper-like in sea lions, seals, and walruses

SPECIES: 38 sea lions, walruses, seals, otters, and polar bears

Mediterranean monk seal

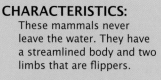

Atlantic spotted dolphins develop their spots only as they grow older. This mother is fully spotted.

These dolphins communicate with squawks, whistles, and buzzes.

This young dolphin, called a calf, is gray-white, with no spots at all. It will be cared for by its mother for up to five years.

MARINE MAMMAL RECORDS

Heaviest and longest: Blue whale, up to 381,000 lb (173,000 kg) and 110 ft (33.6 m) long

Heaviest and longest carnivoran: Southern elephant seal, up to 11,000 lb (5,000 kg) and 22.5 ft (6.8 m) long

Shortest: Marine otter, as small as 34 in (87 cm) long

Fastest swimmer: Common dolphin, up to 40 mph (64 km/h)

Longest living: Bowhead whale, possibly up to 200 years

Blue whale

DID YOU KNOW? All mammals grow hair at some point in their life, but whales and dolphins are completely or nearly hairless as adults.

Marine Reptiles

The first reptiles lived on land, but around 299 to 252 million years ago, some reptiles adapted to life in the ocean. Today, there are around 12,000 species of reptiles, but only about 80 are marine. Reptiles need to breathe air into their lungs, so they come to the surface regularly.

Groups of Marine Reptiles

Marine reptiles belong to three orders. The turtle order contains 7 species of sea turtles. The crocodilian order contains 2 species of crocodiles that swim in the ocean. The squamate order contains 1 species of marine iguana and around 69 species of sea snakes. Squamates have skin protected by small, overlapping scales. Turtles and crocodiles grow harder bony plates called scutes.

Like most reptiles, a saltwater crocodile lays tough-shelled eggs on land. To break out of its shell, the baby uses a horny piece of skin on the tip of its snout called an egg-tooth.

Sea Snakes

Of all marine reptiles, sea snakes are best adapted to life in the ocean. While most marine reptiles have to go ashore to lay eggs and perhaps to rest, the majority of sea snakes never leave the ocean. They even give birth to live, swimming young in the water. Only the sea snakes known as kraits go on land to lay eggs.

It kills eels and other fish by biting with its sharp fangs, which inject a dose of venom.

With its paddle-like tail, the ornate sea snake is an excellent swimmer. Although it must surface eventually to breathe, it can absorb some oxygen from the water through its skin.

DID YOU KNOW? The sea snake with the deadliest venom is the Dubois' sea snake, but luckily it does not inject enough venom to kill a human with a single bite.

The yellow-lipped sea krait returns to land to rest, digest its food, and lay eggs.

This sea krait grows to 4.7 ft (1.42 m) long.

A newly hatched leatherback sea turtle makes its way to the sea.

MARINE REPTILE RECORDS

Heaviest and longest: Saltwater crocodile, up to 3,000 lb (1,360 kg) and 20.7 ft (6.3 m) long

Heaviest and longest turtle: Leatherback sea turtle, up to 1,430 lb (650 kg) and 7 ft (2.1 m) long

Shortest: Marine iguana, as small as 11.4 in (29 cm) long

Fastest swimmer: Leatherback sea turtle, up to 21 mph (35 km/h)

Longest living: Saltwater crocodile, possibly more than 100 years

Seabirds

Around 170 million years ago, birds started to evolve from reptiles called dinosaurs. Like most reptiles, birds lay hard-shelled eggs on land. All birds have wings, a beak, and a covering of feathers. Seabirds find their food beaneath the waves, on the ocean surface, or at the shoreline.

Adapted to the Sea

Seabirds have features that help them survive in and around the ocean. Since too much salt is dangerous for birds, many seabirds have glands in their head to remove the salt they swallow while drinking and eating. Seabird wings may be flipper-like for swimming beneath the surface, or extra-wide for flying great distances over the oceans in search of food. Many seabirds have webbed feet, with skin and tissue joining the toes, making them paddle-like for swimming.

The Atlantic puffin dives as deep as 223 ft (68 m) in search of fish. It uses its short, flipper-like wings as paddles, while steering with its webbed feet.

Careful Parents

Seabirds lay fewer eggs than most other birds, many laying just one egg per year. They also spend longer caring for their chicks, with frigatebirds giving the most time—14 months. Seabirds need a different strategy from landbirds because parenting by the stormy sea is dangerous and exhausting, as parents often travel far in search of food for their chicks. By putting all their energy into fewer chicks, hopefully one will survive.

Blue-footed boobies often have two chicks, but the eggs hatch four or five days apart, so the parents do not have two helpless newborns to care for at once.

The white-tailed sea eagle has the largest wingspan (from wingtip to wingtip) of any eagle, reaching 8 ft (2.45 m). It lives around ocean coasts as well as lakes and rivers.

Like other eagles, this bird has a hooked beak for ripping into its prey.

It uses its sharp claws to snatch fish from near the water surface, usually getting only its feet wet.

SEABIRD RECORDS

Heaviest: Emperor penguin, up to 100 lb (45 kg) and 4.3 ft (1.3 m) tall

Largest wingspan: Wandering albatross, up to 12.1 ft (3.7 m) wide

Shortest: Least storm petrel, as small as 5.1 in (13 cm) long

Fastest swimmer: Gentoo penguin, up to 22 mph (36 km/h)

Longest living: Laysan albatross, possibly more than 66 years

Emperor penguins

DID YOU KNOW? An Arctic tern flies around 1.5 million miles (2.4 million km) in its life, between Arctic coasts in the northern summer and Antarctica in the southern summer.

Food Chains

A food chain is a series of living things that are linked to each other because each feeds on the next in the series. At the top of a food chain is an apex predator, or "top hunter," an animal so big and fierce that it is not usually hunted by anything else.

Making Energy

At the bottom of ocean food chains are the living things that make their own food by turning sunlight into food energy through a process called photosynthesis. These living things are called producers. Many of them are microorganisms such as cyanobacteria, diatoms, and tiny plants. These microorganisms usually cannot move, so they float along near the sunlit water surface. They are called phytoplankton, from the ancient Greek for "plant drifter." Larger producers include plants, such as seagrass, and chromists, such as algae.

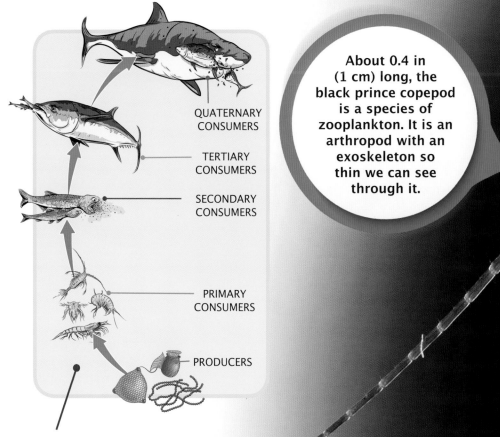

QUATERNARY CONSUMERS

TERTIARY CONSUMERS

SECONDARY CONSUMERS

PRIMARY CONSUMERS

PRODUCERS

About 0.4 in (1 cm) long, the black prince copepod is a species of zooplankton. It is an arthropod with an exoskeleton so thin we can see through it.

This diagram shows an ocean food chain, starting with tiny energy-producers. Not all ocean food chains have the same number of links: For example, some huge animals, such as the blue whale, eat tiny primary consumers.

BIGGEST APEX PREDATORS

Sperm whale: Up to 67.3 ft (20.5 m) long

Orca, also known as the killer whale: Up to 32.2 ft (9.8 m) long

Saltwater crocodile: Up to 20.7 ft (6.3 m) long

Great white shark: Up to 20 ft (6.1 m) long

Tiger shark: Up to 18 ft (5.5 m) long

Tiger shark

It moves by waving these appendages (external body parts), but does not have enough strength to swim against the current.

Passing on Energy

Producers are eaten by plant-eating animals, which passes on the food energy they made. Plant-eaters are called primary consumers. Many of them are tiny floating animals called zooplankton, from the ancient Greek for "animal drifter." Other primary consumers are larger, such as seagrass-eating green turtles. The next level of the chain is carnivores, or meat-eaters, which get their energy from eating plant-eaters. These secondary consumers may be eaten by larger animals, called tertiary consumers, which may be eaten by even larger animals, called quaternary consumers.

This copepod feeds by using its appendages to grab as many as 370,000 phytoplanktons in a day.

The tiny Antarctic krill is an invertebrate that is a key part of food chains in the Southern Ocean. It eats phytoplankton, then is eaten by whales, seals, squid, fish, and penguins.

DID YOU KNOW? There are 300 to 400 trillion Antarctic krill, weighing about 550 million tons (500 million tonnes)—making them the planet's weightiest species.

Predators and Prey

More than half of marine animals are predators, spending much of their time hunting for other animals to eat. Predators have evolved to have features and behaviors that make them good hunters. At the same time, their prey have developed their own special defenses.

Hunting Techniques

There are two main methods of catching prey: Ambush and pursuit. Ambush predators sit and wait for prey, then pounce at the last moment. Ambush predators are often well camouflaged, so they blend into their environment. Some burrow into the ocean floor or hide in crevices. Pursuit predators, such as dolphins, chase after their prey, so they must be fast.

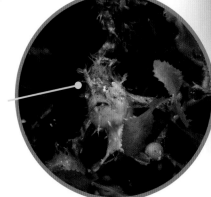

The sargassum fish is a well–camouflaged ambush predator that lives among sargassum seaweed. It uses a long growth on its head as a "lure" to attract fish and shrimp, then sucks them into its mouth.

MEGA–SHOALS

Estimated shoal size

Atlantic herring: Up to 4 billion fish

Pacific sardine: Up to 300 million fish

Peruvian anchovy: Up to 100 million fish

Atlantic mackerel: Up to 1 million fish

A sardine shoal

DID YOU KNOW? Spinner dolphins work together to capture fish, circling a shoal and then moving slowly inward until the fish are tightly packed.

Defensive Techniques

One way to avoid being eaten is to go unnoticed, so many marine animals are camouflaged, while others are active only at night. Another defensive method is to live in a group. Some fish move in groups called shoals, giving them a greater chance of spotting predators and cutting down the chance of any single fish being eaten. Some animals make themselves difficult to catch or eat: Octopus distract predators by releasing clouds of dark ink, while some sea urchins are covered in sharp spines. A few animals, such as pufferfish, are poisonous, so no predator will try the species twice.

The mimic octopus has a very unusual defense: It positions and moves its body to pretend to be more dangerous species, such as sea snakes. This one is pretending to be a poisonous flatfish.

This pipefish is almost transparent, but over a few hours it can change its color to match a new background.

Its camouflage is useful as a defense and while waiting to ambush shrimp, which it sucks into its tube-shaped mouth.

Ocean Life at Risk

Human activities have damaged ocean habitats and reduced the numbers of many ocean species. As a result, around 2,270 marine animals are at risk of extinction. Many of these animals are called "endangered" species, while those very close to being wiped out are "critically endangered."

Damaged Habitats

When humans burn fuels such as coal and oil, we release "greenhouse gases" such as carbon dioxide into the atmosphere. These gases trap the Sun's heat and raise the Earth's temperature, like in a glass greenhouse. This global warming is slowly heating the oceans, making ice melt at the poles and damaging coral reefs. Other habitat damage is caused by rubbish, spills of chemicals, and building along coasts, which can destroy nesting sites.

The smalltooth sawfish lives along warm coasts of the Atlantic Ocean. It is critically endangered by habitat damage and fishing. This baby was born in an aquarium and is being released into the ocean to help grow the numbers of wild sawfish.

The Atlantic cod was overfished in the 1990s, so today governments set limits on how many fish can be caught.

Hunting and Fishing

Some marine animals have been driven to extinction by human hunting, including the Atlantic Ocean gray whales, which died out in the eighteenth century. Today, the hunting of whales and other threatened species is banned by most countries. However, fish that are often eaten by humans can still suffer from overfishing. This is when so many fish are caught that the remaining adults cannot have babies fast enough to maintain the species.

Although it is illegal to hunt the critically endangered Kemp's ridley sea turtle, it is often accidentally trapped and killed in nets for catching shrimp.

Using its lips, the wrasse carries sea urchins to a rock, where it cracks them open.

Some female wrasses turn into males at around nine years old, probably because older, bigger males can father more babies than older females can produce.

A pair of mating Cape gannets greet each other.

THREATENED SEABIRDS

Of around 1,500 threatened bird species

Balearic shearwater: Construction of hotels in its island habitat

Cape gannet: Lack of food due to human overfishing

Northern rockhopper penguin: Global warming, pollution, and overfishing

Spoonbilled sandpiper: Loss of its coastal habitats to industry

Waved albatross: Accidental capture in fishing lines

DID YOU KNOW? Water expands as it gets warmer, so scientists predict that sea levels will rise by anything from 10 in to 8.8 ft (26 to 270 cm) by the year 2100.

Ocean Zones

All living things are adapted to their surroundings, or habitat. In the ocean, the two key things that affect habitat are sunlight and temperature. Animals and plants that live in bright, warm waters could not survive in the darkest, coldest depths.

Temperature Zones

The ocean is warmest close to the equator, where it is heated most strongly by the Sun's rays. All over the world, surface waters are warmer than the waters beneath, as sunlight cannot penetrate farther than 3,300 ft (1,000 m) into the deep.

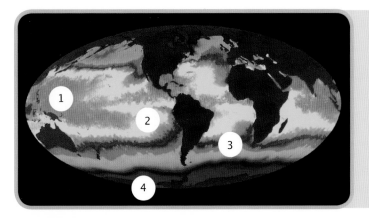

Ocean Climates

This map shows the average temperature at the water surface, from warm (red) to cold (blue).

KEY

1. **Tropical:** Water warm year round

2. **Subtropical:** Water fairly warm year round

3. **Temperate:** Water ranges from cold to warm

4. **Polar:** Water cold year round

Depth Zones

The sunlit surface waters are rich with life. Here, plants and chromists make their food from sunlight. These provide food for plant-eaters, which are eaten in their turn by bigger species. In the deep, dark ocean, there is no plant life and far fewer animals.

1. **SUNLIGHT ZONE:**
   0 to 660 ft (0 to 200 m)
   Most ocean plants and animals live here.

2. **TWILIGHT ZONE:**
   660 to 3,300 ft (200 to 1,000 m)
   Some animals travel from these dim waters to feed near the surface at night.

3. **MIDNIGHT ZONE:**
   3,300 to 13,000 ft (1,000 to 4,000 m)
   In total darkness, many animals are bioluminescent, or make their own light.

4. **ABYSSAL ZONE:**
   13,000 ft (4,000 m) to ocean floor
   Most animals have special features to survive the cold.

5. **HADAL ZONE:**
   Deep trenches
   Only a few species are known to survive here.

DEPTH AND TEMPERATURE RECORDS

Deepest trench: Mariana Trench, Pacific Ocean, 36,201 ft (11,034 m)

Shallowest ocean: Arctic Ocean, average depth 3,406 ft (1,038 m)

Coldest water: 28.4°F (−2°C), Arctic and Southern Oceans

Hottest water: 95°F (35°C), in summer on the coasts of the Persian Gulf, Indian Ocean

Abu Dhabi, Persian Gulf

Many ocean animals are suited to a small range of temperatures and depths. Bigeye tuna are unusual because they can survive in deeper, colder waters and warm surface waters.

The bigeye tuna descends and rises as it follows its prey, such as sardines.

Its large eyes enable the tuna to see when it swims as deep as 1,650 ft (500 m).

DID YOU KNOW? Seawater turns to ice tr at 28.4°F (−2°C) because the salt lowers its freezing point below that of freshwater (32°F/0°C).

Beaches

Sandy or muddy beaches are challenging habitats. Animals and plants must survive being plunged underwater by rising tides and breaking waves, then being exposed to the Sun and wind as the water draws back.

Tides

All beaches have daily high tides, when the sea washes up the shore, and low tides, when the sea draws back out. Tides are caused by gravity. Gravity pulls all objects toward each other, with larger objects, like planets and moons, having the greatest pull. As the Moon pulls on Earth, the sea bulges toward it. As the Earth turns, the moving bulge creates rising and falling tides.

This sand hopper burrows into the sand during high tide, but comes out when the tide is low to feed on washed-up seaweed.

Surviving the Intertidal Zone

Animals living in the intertidal zone, the area between the high and low tide lines, have to survive dramatic changes in their habitat. Some beach animals, such as birds, move up the beach when the tide rises. Others burrow into the sand, choosing wet sand if they need to stay damp. Some insects, such as dune chafer and sandgraver beetles, shelter in the seaweed and driftwood found at the high tide line.

The lugworm burrows in damp sand. It eats sand, digesting the microorganisms it contains, then poops out a coiled "cast" of used sand.

SANDERLING

Length: 7 to 8 in (18 to 21 cm)

Range: Arctic in summer; Americas, Africa, Europe, Asia, and Australasia in winter

Habitat: Sandy and rocky beaches

Diet: Buried invertebrates, including arthropods, mollusks, and worms

Conservation: Not at risk

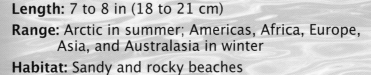

A sanderling pulls a bloodworm from the sand.

This crab lives on tropical beaches of the Indian and Pacific Oceans.

The horn-eyed ghost crab's eyes are on stalks, which can be folded down when it is burrowing.

The crab uses its claws to burrow into the sand, so it can hide during the day.

DID YOU KNOW? Tiny mole crabs can completely bury themselves under sand in just 1.5 seconds.

Rocky Shores

Sea cliffs offer resting and nesting spaces for many species of seabirds. On rocky beaches, battered by the waves, lots of animals have hard shells for protection. Many of them attach to the rocks so they are not dragged out to sea.

Clinging On

Hard-shelled invertebrates are often found clinging to rocks and other surfaces in the intertidal zone. These include bivalves, such as mussels and oysters, which have two-part shells that open and close for protection. They use a muscly foot to dig into the seafloor or they attach themselves to rocks with a sticky thread called byssus. Other groups of clingers-on include the single-shelled limpets and the barnacles, with shells usually made of six plates.

Pale-shelled goose barnacles and blue mussels wait for the tide to rise, so they can feed on tiny creatures in the water.

Limpets are snails that move by rippling the muscles of their foot. When the tide is low, they attach themselves tightly to rocks so they do not dry out.

Invertebrates in this rock pool include ochre starfish, purple sea urchins, and sea anemones.

Rock Pools

At low tide, pools of water are left behind in dips and crevices in the rocks. The animals, plants, and chromists that live in them must be able to survive sudden changes in temperature, blasts of wind, and drying out in the sun. If the pool empties, green algae may provide the only shelter, as seabirds swoop to find food.

SEA SLATER

Length: 1 to 1.2 in (2.5 to 3 cm)

Range: Temperate coasts of Europe and North America

Habitat: Rock pools and crevices on rocky beaches

Diet: Seaweed and diatoms

Conservation: Not at risk

Sea slater

Common murres spend most of their lives at sea, returning to land only to nest on rocky cliffs.

Murres nest in large colonies, or groups, which are known as loomeries.

These seabirds use their wings to "swim" underwater as they chase cod and herring.

DID YOU KNOW? There are at least 12,000 species of seaweeds, which are plant–like organisms known as algae.

Mangrove Forests

Mangroves are trees that can live in saltwater. They are often found along tropical and subtropical coasts where the water is shallow and calm. Fish and invertebrates shelter among the mangroves' roots, while birds perch on branches as they watch for prey.

Archerfish

In a mangrove forest, ocean meets land in a unique habitat. Archerfish are among the species that have evolved to make full use of this mix. These fish catch insects that are sitting on branches overhanging the water by firing jets of water at them. Archerfish do this by sucking in water, pressing their tongue against the roof of their mouth to form a tube, then spitting.

Red mangroves are among the most common species of mangrove trees.

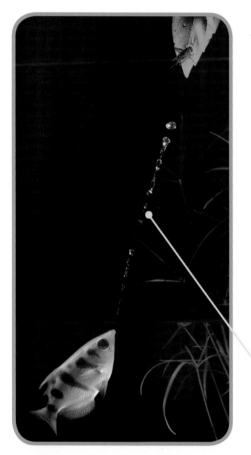

A banded archerfish shoots a jet of water at a cricket. When the cricket falls into the water, it will be snapped up.

Mudskippers

These fish have developed extraordinary features that enable them to survive in the intertidal zone of mangrove forests. At low tide, mudskippers use their strong pectoral fins to drag themselves across the exposed mud. While most fish cannot breathe out of water, mudskippers can soak up oxygen from the air through their skin, as long as they stay wet by rolling in puddles.

A mudskipper's eyes move separately from each other, so the fish can see above and below water at the same time.

DID YOU KNOW? The banded archerfish can aim jets of water at prey sitting up to 9.8 ft (3 m) away.

Long, stilt-like roots enable the mangroves' branches and leaves to stay above the level of high tide.

Mangroves are often "nurseries" for young fish, which find hiding places and plenty of food among the roots and mud.

Mangrove pitta

MANGROVE PITTA

Length: 7 to 8.3 in (18 to 21 cm)

Range: Coasts of southern Asia

Habitat: Mangrove forests

Diet: Small crabs, snails, and insects

Conservation: Population shrinking due to habitat loss

Kelp Forests

Kelps are plant-like algae that grow in cool, coastal waters. Where kelps grow thickly, they form a habitat called a kelp forest. These provide shelter from storms; hiding places from predators; and food for plant-eaters, which are in turn food for meat-eaters.

Giant kelp grows to more than 160 ft (50 m) long.

A Vital Habitat

Like an above-water forest of trees, kelp forests have a "canopy" formed by the tallest species, which grow up to the water surface. In the shade beneath, shorter species form a thick "understory" and carpet the seafloor. Invertebrates, such as sea urchins, feed on the kelp itself. They are preyed on by kelp bass and other fish. These smaller creatures are food for mammals including seals, sea lions, otters, and gray whales. Birds such as gulls and cormorants swoop at the surface.

The kelp bass lives in kelp forests, where it feeds on small fish, squid, and shrimp.

A bat ray swims through a kelp forest off the coast of California, USA.

WESTERN SPINY BRITTLE STAR

Length: 7 to 15 in (18 to 38 cm)

Range: Pacific Ocean from southern USA to Peru

Habitat: Sandy seafloor, often around kelp, to depths of 6,500 ft (2,000 m)

Diet: Small invertebrates and microorganisms

Conservation: Not at risk

Western spiny brittle stars

DID YOU KNOW? Growing at up to 2 ft (60 cm) per day, giant kelp is one of the fastest-growing living things in the world.

Kelp anchors itself in the seabed with a root-like structure called a "holdfast."

With strips of kelp on its back, this graceful decorator crab is hoping to hide from predators such as sea otters.

Decorator Crabs

Many animals hide away in kelp forests, but the graceful decorator crab uses a more unusual form of camouflage. It attaches kelp and other living things, such as sponges, to hooks on its shell, so it can disguise itself.

Seagrass Meadows

There are around 60 species of seagrasses, which can cover the seafloor rather like meadows of grass on land. These plants need sunlight to photosynthesize, so they grow in clear, shallow waters. They are found from the equator nearly all the way to the North and South Poles.

Fish Nurseries

Many fish use seagrass meadows as nurseries, where eggs are released and young fish can grow safely, hiding from predators among the grass. When the fish grow into adults, many swim away to a range of habitats, from nearby coral reefs to the vast ocean. Other fish, often small and well-camouflaged species such as seahorses, stay among the seagrass for life.

Precious Habitat

Hundreds of species, from green turtles and manatees to sea urchins, feed on seagrass leaves and stems. Other animals use the grass as a hiding place as they lie in wait for prey. Among these ambush predators are fish such as the fierce and well-camouflaged moray eels and grass gobies. However, pollution and coastal construction are destroying seagrass meadows at a rate of two football fields every hour. Today, one-quarter of seagrass animals are at risk.

Found in the tropical Indian and Pacific Oceans, a young blue triggerfish is sheltered by seagrass.

Adult green sea turtles spend most of their time grazing in seagrass meadows.

A snowflake moray eel watches for shrimp and small crabs. It will snap them up with its powerful jaws, crushing their shells with its blunt teeth, then use an extra set of teeth, in its throat, for mashing them.

FLORAL BLENNY

Length: 3.1 to 3.3 in (8 to 8.5 cm)

Range: Tropical coasts of the Indian and Pacific Oceans

Habitat: Seagrass meadows and coral reefs

Diet: Algae, diatoms, and small crustaceans

Conservation: Population at risk in some regions

Floral blenny

The green sea turtle can grow to 5 ft (1.5 m) long.

The destruction of seagrass meadows, along with hunting and pollution, have put this turtle at risk of extinction.

DID YOU KNOW? The green sea turtle gets its name from the layer of green fat under its shell, caused by eating so much seagrass.

Coral Reefs

Coral reefs are home to one-quarter of all marine species. Reefs are rocky ridges built by stony corals. These invertebrates live in large groups called colonies. Reefs are found in shallow, tropical waters. Some coral species live in cold, deep water, but they do not build great reefs.

Building Reefs

Reefs are made of the skeletons of millions or billions of stony coral polyps. A polyp has a soft, cuplike body, armed with tentacles for catching food. Each polyp builds a hard skeleton around itself. When a polyp dies, its skeleton is left behind and a new polyp settles on top, growing the reef. Today, around two-thirds of coral reefs are at risk, as they are very sensitive to water temperature and pollution.

Up to 7 in (18 cm) long, the mirror butterflyfish feeds on coral polyps and small invertebrates.

Brain corals are among more than 3,000 species of stony corals. Each brain coral is a colony of thousands of tiny, identical living polyps.

DID YOU KNOW? The world's largest coral reef system is the Great Barrier Reef, which stretches for over 1,400 miles (2,300 km) off the coast of Australia.

This is a soft coral colony, made up of tiny polyps that do not build a hard skeleton. Polyps are food for reef fish and invertebrates.

Bright Shades

Many reef fish and invertebrates are brightly colored and patterned. For some, such as spotted trunkfish, the pattern warns other animals they are poisonous. Predators come to link that pattern with danger. Bright patterns are also useful for picking out other members of the same species for mating. For most reef species, their colors and patterns act as camouflage against the colorful, sun-dappled reef.

This day octopus is totally still as it waits for fish, crabs, or shrimp. In just a few seconds, it changes the color and patterns on its skin to match the surrounding coral.

The emperor angelfish has bright blue and yellow stripes. It eats hard-to-chew sponges and algae with its large, strong jaws.

COPPERBAND BUTTERFLYFISH

Length: 7 to 8 in (18 to 20 cm)

Range: Tropical coasts of the Indian and Pacific Oceans

Habitat: Coral reefs and rocky shores

Diet: Sea anenomes, worms, and mollusks

Conservation: Not at risk

Copperband butterflyfish

Polar Waters

In winter, the surface of the Arctic Ocean and the sea surrounding Antarctica freezes. In summer, this sea ice melts and shrinks. Platforms of ice as thick as 3,300 ft (1,000 m), called ice shelves, extend into the ocean from the land. Sometimes, icebergs break off and float away.

Staying Warm

Animals that live in the Arctic and Southern Oceans must have special features to survive the cold. Mammals, such as seals and whales, have a thick layer of fat called blubber, which keeps in their body heat. They also have rounded bodies, with a smaller surface from which to lose heat. This has the same warming effect as huddling into a ball. Polar seabirds have a waterproof coat of tightly packed feathers.

Up to 7.5 ft (2.3 m) long, crabeater seals rest and mate on the sea ice around Antarctica.

Anti-Freeze Blood

Fish that live in the coldest waters need special defenses to stop their blood from freezing. Antarctic icefish blood contains a special substance called glycoprotein. It disturbs the molecules in the blood, stopping them from joining together and freezing into ice.

The blood of an icefish is thin and colorless, which makes the fish transparent.

Narwhals are toothed whales that live in the Arctic Ocean, feeding on fish beneath the sea ice.

ARCTIC TERN

Length: 11 to 15 in (28 to 39 cm)

Range: Arctic and northern temperate coasts in northern summer; Southern Ocean and coasts in southern summer

Habitat: Coasts, grassland, and oceans

Diet: Small fish, crabs, and krill

Conservation: Population shrinking due to habitat loss and overfishing

Arctic tern

Narwhals live in groups of up to 20, joining together into groups of up to 1,000 in summer.

Male narwhals have a spiral tusk up to 10.2 ft (3.1 m) long. It is a tooth that grows from the left side of the mouth, through the lip.

DID YOU KNOW? The bowhead whale, which lives in the Arctic Ocean, has the thickest blubber of any animal, up to 20 in (50 cm) thick.

Deep Ocean

In the midnight zone, the temperature is only around 39°F (4°C). With no light, there are no plants and no plant-eating animals. Many animals here are predators that hunt by smell and touch rather than by sight and speed. Some eat the dead plants and animals that sink to the seafloor.

Strange Bodies

Fish that spend some of their time in the twilight zone have huge eyes that can gather as much light as possible. Fish that never leave the midnight zone may be completely eyeless but have fins that are very sensitive to touch. Below 3,300 ft (1,000 m), many fish have small bodies, which need little food, and large mouths and stomachs to swallow whatever prey comes their way.

A gulper eel's huge mouth can open wide enough to swallow prey much larger than the eel itself.

HALF-NAKED HATCHETFISH

Length: 1.2 to 2 in (3 to 5 cm)

Range: Tropical to temperate Atlantic, Indian, and Pacific Oceans

Habitat: From depths of 650 to 7,870 ft (200 to 2,400 m)

Diet: Zooplankton

Conservation: Not at risk

Half-naked hatchetfish

Bioluminescence

Many deep-sea fish can make their own light, using light-producing organs called photophores. Some, including anglerfish, use long bioluminescent growths to attract prey. Others, such as hatchetfish, use bioluminesence as a defensive method called counterillumination. By lighting their undersides, they are less visible from below, when seen against the lighter water above.

This female triplewart seadevil, a species of anglerfish, tries to lure fish and invertebrates. Male seadevils are only 0.4 in (1 cm) long and feed by attaching themselves to a female.

Günther's lanternfish lives in the Atlantic Ocean.

Photophores produce blue light, used for counterillumination and to signal to other members of the species.

This lanternfish lives in the twilight zone during the day, climbing to the sunlight zone at night to feed on zooplankton.

DID YOU KNOW? The scaly dragonfish, which lives as deep as 4,900 ft (1,500 m), can turn its bioluminescence on and off to confuse predators.

Hydrothermal Vents

The Earth's surface is made from giant plates of rock that move slowly against each other, sometimes causing earthquakes and volcanoes. Hydrothermal vents are cracks in the seafloor, above the plate edges. Water heated in the Earth's super-hot interior rises through the vents.

Hotspots for Life

A hydrothermal vent offers a completely different habitat from the surrounding seafloor. The water from a vent ranges from 140°F to 860°F (60°C to 460°C). The water is also rich in minerals, such as sulfur, from inside the Earth. Special bacteria use the sulfur to make their own food. Other animals, most of them found only around vents, eat the bacteria and each other.

This vent is 10,800 ft (3,300 m) below the surface of the Atlantic Ocean. It is called a "black smoker" because minerals in the water have slowly built rocky chimneys, which belch out black, sulfur–rich water.

Giant tube worms attach themselves to the seabed. Their red "plume," which collects sulfur from the water, is pulled inside the protective tube if a predator arrives.

Giant Tube Worms

Giant tube worms live only around sulfur-rich vents on the Pacific Ocean floor. They get their food by taking bacteria into their skin, rather like getting an infection. The bacteria make their home inside the worms, where they turn sulfur into food, which the worms share.

HYDROTHERMAL THREE-BEARDED ROCKLING

Length: 10 to 12 in (25 to 30 cm)

Range: Lucky Strike Vents, Mid-Atlantic Ridge, Atlantic Ocean

Habitat: From depths of 300 to 5,500 ft (900 to 1,700 m) around vents

Diet: Shrimp and other invertebrates

Conservation: Not at risk

Known to scientists as *Gaidropsarus mauli*, this species was discovered in 2018.

Galatheid crabs feed on bacteria.

Using remote-controlled submarines, researchers have discovered many new species of shrimp living around hydrothermal vents.

These hydrothermal mussels have attached to the seafloor beside the Champagne Vent, on the floor of the Pacific Ocean.

DID YOU KNOW? Giant tube worms, which live in colonies of many hundred worms, can grow to 7.9 ft (2.4 m) long.

Anthozoa

Anthozoa include sea anemones and corals, as well as sea pens, fans, and whips. Corals are in two main groups: the soft corals and the stony corals, which build the hard skeletons that form coral reefs. Apart from sea anemones, which live alone, most anthozoans live in groups called colonies.

Life Cycle

Adult anthozoans are called polyps. They are tube-shaped, with a central mouth surrounded by tentacles for grabbing prey. For anthozoans that live alone, each polyp attaches to the seafloor with its foot. For anthozoans that live in colonies, the foot attaches to other, identical polyps. Young anthozoans, called larvae, have simpler body shapes. They swim along till they are ready to settle down and grow into adults.

A sea fan is a colony of thousands of tiny polyps, each with eight tentacles.

Sea Anemones

A sea anemone polyp has tens or hundreds of tentacles, which are armed with stinging cells. If the cells are touched, they shoot out an arrow-like structure that sticks into the prey or predator, injecting them with venom. The venom paralyzes prey, so it can be moved easily to the anenome's mouth.

Living on the deep ocean floor, the Venus flytrap sea anemone closes its tentacles to trap prey or to protect itself from predators.

The common clownfish lives among the tentacles of carpet sea anemones, where it is well-hidden from predators.

The anemone benefits from hosting clownfish because they scare away other fish, such as butterflyfish, that would nibble their tentacles.

Clownfish are covered in thick mucus that protects them from anemone stings.

SHORT-QUILL SEA PEN

Length: 12 to 16 in (30 to 40 cm)

Range: Tropical Indian and Pacific Oceans

Habitat: Sandy or muddy seabed in shallow, coastal waters

Diet: Plankton

Conservation: Not at risk

A short-quill sea pen colony is symmetrical.

DID YOU KNOW? There are more than 6,000 species of anthozoans, ranging from single polyps just 0.4 in (1 cm) across to colonies more than 3.3 ft (1 m) across.

Jellyfish

Despite their name, jellyfish are not fish but invertebrates related to anthozoans. Adult jellyfish have soft bodies with an umbrella-shaped "bell" and long tentacles. They swim by expanding and squeezing their bell, pushing water behind them.

Changing Body

A jellyfish starts life as a tiny, floating larva. When the larva finds a rock or other surface, it attaches to it and starts to grow into a polyp. Jellyfish polyps look like anthozoan polyps, with a central mouth and tentacles for catching prey. After a few weeks or months, the polyp starts budding: Its body breaks off into baby jellyfish, which swim away. These grow into adult jellyfish, called medusae. Medusae release eggs that grow into larvae.

Stinging Tentacles

Jellyfish tentacles have stinging cells that can stun or kill prey. Jellyfish may catch prey by trailing their tentacles behind them or sinking through the water with their tentacles spread wide. When prey is within reach, the tentacles direct it to the mouth, in the center of the bell.

The golden jellyfish lives only in Jellyfish Lake, on the island of Eil Malk in the Pacific Ocean.

The bell of a lion's mane jellyfish medusa can grow as wide as 7.5 ft (2.3 m).

The moon jellyfish uses its tentacles to catch zooplankton.

The seawater lake is connected to the ocean by tunnels.

Thousands of golden jellyfish swim across the lake together every day.

Crowned jellyfish

CROWNED JELLYFISH

Length: 30 to 33 in (75 to 85 cm)

Range: Tropical Atlantic, Indian, and Pacific Oceans

Habitat: Open ocean

Diet: Plankton, algae, shrimp, and eggs

Conservation: Not at risk

DID YOU KNOW? Jellyfish do not have eyes or a brain, but they respond to messages from their nerves, which sense touch and heat.

Octopus and Squid

Octopus and squid are cephalopods, a group of 800 species that also includes nautilus and cuttlefish. Cephalopods have large heads and eyes, as well as arms or tentacles. Most of them have an ink sac, which can release a cloud of dark ink to confuse predators.

Moving Along

Octopus have eight arms covered with suckers, which they use to hold prey. Squid also have eight suckered arms, plus two long tentacles for grabbing. Octopus and squid can swim very fast by sucking in water, then pushing it out through a tube-shaped body part called a siphon. The animal moves in the opposite direction to the jet of water. Octopus can also crawl along the seafloor, while squid can swim gently by waving their fins.

The bigfin reef squid's skin is covered in color-changing cells. It uses these to control its body color and pattern.

Intelligent Invertebrates

Cephalopods have large brains and are the most intelligent of all invertebrates. They show this through a number of skills. Some octopus signal to each other by changing their body color, while Humboldt squid work together to capture prey. Several species of octopus, including blue-ringed octopus, use rocks and other objects to build dens.

SOUTHERN BOBTAIL SQUID

Length: 2.4 to 2.8 in (6 to 7 cm)

Range: Temperate coasts of Australia

Habitat: Seagrass meadows and sandy or muddy seafloors in shallow water

Diet: Shrimp and fish

Conservation: Not known

The southern bobtail squid is bioluminescent.

When the octopus feels threatened, the rings on its skin turn bright blue to frighten away predators.

This coconut octopus is walking on two "legs" as it carries a shell to hide inside.

Although all octopus have a venomous bite, only blue-ringed octopus make a venom so deadly it can kill humans.

DID YOU KNOW? The smallest cephalopods are pygmy squid, which grow little more than 0.4 in (1 cm) long.

Crabs

Crabs belong to a group of arthropods called crustaceans. Like all arthropods, including insects and spiders, they have a tough exoskeleton and jointed legs, which bend easily for walking. Unlike other arthropods, crustaceans have two pairs of feelers, called antennae, on their heads.

Ten Legs

Crabs have five pairs of legs. The back four pairs are for walking, often in a sidewise direction because of their position and joints, but sometimes forward or backward. The front pair of legs, often called claws, end in pincers. The claws are used for grabbing and killing prey, as well as for signaling and fighting.

Male fiddler crabs have one claw much larger than the other. They use it for signaling to females and for fighting off other males so they can win a mate.

Hermit Crabs

Although hermit crabs are crustaceans, they are not true crabs. True crabs have a very tough shell covering their body, called a carapace. Hermit crabs do not have a carapace, so they protect their soft body using the empty shell of another creature, often a sea snail.

Hermit crabs carry around an abandoned seashell, then pull their whole body inside at the first sign of danger.

HALLOWEEN CRAB

Length: 4 to 4.7 in (10 to 12 cm)

Range: Pacific coast of Central America

Habitat: Mangrove forest, sand dunes, coastal rainforest, and shallow ocean

Diet: Leaves and young plants

Conservation: Not at risk

Halloween crab

The red rock crab lives on rocky seashores in Central and South America.

The carapace is around 3 in (8 cm) long.

Like other beach-living crabs, the female red rock crab releases her larvae into the water. When the larvae have grown into adults, they swim ashore.

DID YOU KNOW? The largest crab is the Japanese spider crab, which reaches 12 ft (3.8 m) from pincer to pincer but has a carapace only 1.3 ft (0.4 m) wide.

Lobsters and Relatives

Lobsters and shrimp are all crustaceans with ten legs. In addition to their legs, they have several other pairs of appendages, or long body parts, including antennae and mouthparts. All these crustaceans have bodies that are segmented, or divided into parts.

Clawed Lobsters

True lobsters have claws on their first three pairs of legs, with the front pair having the biggest claws of all. They spend their life on the seafloor, hiding in crevices or burrows and coming out to catch fish, mollusks, and worms. Although lobsters have eyes, which are usually on stalks, it is murky on the seafloor, so they hunt by using their antennae to sense the chemical "smells" given off by prey.

Found on coral reefs in the Indian and Pacific Oceans, the harlequin shrimp feeds on starfish.

Sometimes weighing more than 44 lb (20 kg), the American lobster is the world's heaviest crustacean.

Spiny Lobsters

Spiny lobsters, which are clawless, have thick and spiny antennae. These antennae play a special role during migration. Every autumn, groups of Caribbean and California spiny lobsters walk across the seafloor from cold and stormy shallow waters into warm and calm deeper waters. The lobsters walk one behind the other, draping their antennae over the lobster in front.

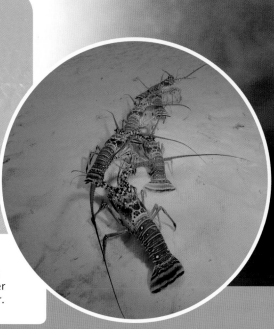

Migrating around 25 miles (40 km), Caribbean spiny lobsters form a line to make pushing through the water easier for all the lobsters except the leader.

PINK SHRIMP

Length: 1.6 to 2 in (4 to 5 cm)

Range: Arctic Ocean and northern Atlantic Ocean

Habitat: Ocean floor at depths of 65 to 330 ft (20 to 100 m)

Diet: Small invertebrates such as crustaceans and worms

Conservation: Not at risk

Pink shrimp

The petal–like antennae are used for "smelling" prey.

The harlequin shrimp's eyes are on short stalks.

These large, flat claws are used for attracting a mate.

DID YOU KNOW? As they grow, crustaceans must shed their exoskeleton, then grow a new one, to make room for their larger body.

Bivalves

Bivalves are soft-bodied animals that live in a tough shell. The shell is in two halves joined by a hinge, so it can open and close. Bivalves include clams, cockles, mussels, and oysters. Many bivalves bury themselves in the sand or mud of the seafloor, while others attach to rocks.

Filter Feeders

Most bivalves eat tiny algae and other small living things using a method called filter feeding. Water is sucked inside the shell, often through a tube called the "inhalant siphon." The water passes through the bivalve's gills, which are covered in sticky mucus. Bits of food stick to the mucus. The used water is pumped out, often through another tube, the "exhalant siphon."

This cockle has stuck out its pink foot, which it uses for burrowing into the seabed. It can also jump by bending and straightening its foot.

Making Pearls

Bivalves make their own shells, using a mineral called calcium carbonate. Some oysters and mussels make a form of calcium carbonate called nacre, which is iridescent, or shines in the colors of the rainbow. They also make pearls out of the same material. When a grain of sand or tiny parasite enters their shell, the bivalve surrounds the intruder with layers of nacre, forming a pearl.

A pearl oyster has lined its shell and made a pearl from iridescent nacre.

DID YOU KNOW? The world's largest pearl, formed inside a giant clam, measures 67 cm (26 in) long and weighs 75 lb (34 kg).

FLAME
SCALLOP

Length: 2.4 to 3.1 in (6 to 8 cm)

Range: Caribbean Sea, in the Atlantic Ocean

Habitat: Seafloor on coral reefs

Diet: Phytoplankton

Conservation: Not at risk

Giant clams live on coral reefs in the Indian and Pacific Oceans.

Giant clams can measure as much as 54 in (137 cm) across and live for over 100 years.

After filter feeding on plankton, the clam pumps out used water through the exhalant siphon.

Sea Slugs and Snails

Slugs and snails are gastropods. They have a head, with two or four tentacles equipped with eyes, and a long foot, which they use to crawl over the seafloor or ground. Around half of the 60,000 species of gastropods live in oceans, while the rest live in freshwater or on land.

This purple-lined nudibranch lives on coral reefs in the tropical Indian and Pacific Oceans.

Shell or No Shell

Gastropods with a shell are usually called snails, while those without a shell are called slugs. Sea snails are often given names like cowry, conch, limpet, and periwinkle. Their shell usually has a spiral shape and is large enough for the animal to pull its whole body inside for protection. Sea slugs are often called nudibranchs.

The tulip snail crawls over the seabed in search of bivalves or other mollusks to attack with its radula, which is a long tongue covered in tiny teeth. The radula is sharp enough to bore through shells.

FLAMINGO TONGUE SNAIL

Length: 0.7 to 1.7 in (1.8 to 4.4 cm)

Range: Tropical western Atlantic Ocean

Habitat: Soft corals in shallow water

Diet: Soft corals

Conservation: Population shrinking due to capture by tourists

The flamingo tongue snail covers its shell with flaps of patterned body tissue.

DID YOU KNOW? Nudibranchs are hermaphrodites, which means they have both male and female body parts, but they still have to find another nudibranch to mate with.

The nudibranch takes oxygen from the water through its frondy gills.

The tentacles are sensitive to touch, taste, and smell.

Nudibranchs

Since nudibranchs do not have a shell, they have evolved other methods of protection. Many nudibranchs eat stinging or bad-tasting animals, such as sea anemones and sponges. Without harming themselves, these nudibranchs store their prey's nasty chemicals in their own bodies. Some nudibranchs can make their own bad-tasting chemicals. If a predator makes the mistake of eating a nudibranch, they will remember not to do it again.

The opalescent nudibranch feeds on stinging sea anemones. Its bright colors act as a warning sign to predators that it is bad to eat.

Starfish

Also known as sea stars, starfish live on the ocean floor, from the shore to the depths. They are radially symmetrical, which means they usually have five equal parts arranged around their center, like slices of a pie. Although most starfish have five arms, some have over fifty.

Creeping Predators

Starfish prey on other seafloor animals, particularly invertebrates. The starfish's mouth is in the middle of its underside. Many starfish can hunt prey much larger than their mouth. When they find prey, they move on top of it and push their stomach out through their mouth, inside-out. The stomach makes digestive fluids to break down the prey. After a while, the stomach and the partly digested prey are pulled inside.

This crown-of-thorns starfish has climbed onto coral and stuck out its stomach. It is turning the coral polyps to mush.

Tube Feet

The undersides of a starfish's arms have many tube-shaped growths called tube feet. Starfish creep slowly across the seafloor by waving their tube feet, which stick to surfaces, with one part of an arm attaching to a surface as another lets go.

The ochre starfish is often seen on wave-washed rocks. As well as being used for movement, its strong tube feet can open the shells of bivalves.

COMMON SUNSTAR

Length: 8 to 14 in (20 to 35 cm)

Range: Arctic and northern Atlantic and Pacific Oceans

Habitat: Rocky seafloor from shore rock pools to depths of 985 ft (300 m)

Diet: Starfish, sea urchins, bivalves, and sea squirts

Conservation: Population shrinking due to global warming

Common sunstar

Found in shallow waters of the Indian and Pacific Oceans, the red knob starfish grows to about 12 in (30 cm) wide.

If it loses one of its arms, this starfish can slowly grow a new one.

At the tip of each arm is an eyespot, which enables the starfish to see light and dark shapes.

DID YOU KNOW? A single crown-of-thorns starfish can eat up to 65 sq ft (6 sq m) of coral reef every year.

Sea Cucumbers and Urchins

Like their relatives the starfish, sea cucumbers and sea urchins are echinoderms. The 7,000 members of this group are found only in the oceans, usually on the seafloor. Adult echinoderms are radially symmetrical and have tough, often spiny, skin.

Sea Cucumbers

Named for their cucumber-shaped body, these echinoderms have a mouth surrounded by tentacles at one end, so—unlike starfish and urchins—they are usually seen lying on their side. They use their tentacles for catching plankton or digging in sand and mud for waste to eat. While most sea cucumbers crawl across the seafloor on their tube feet, some can push themselves off the bottom and float along.

The red-lined sea cucumber has many hard spikes for protection. When threatened, it curls into a ball.

Sea Urchins

These round and spiny echinoderms live on the seafloor, from rock pools to 16,000 ft (5,000 m) deep. Some sea urchins have venomous spines. Like all echinoderms, they do not have a brain, but they have nerves that are sensitive to touch, light, and chemical "smells" in the water. When one of their spines is touched, all the spines move to point at the predator.

Smelling algae to eat, these red and purple sea urchins have crawled across the rock on their tube feet.

CHOCOLATE CHIP SEA CUCUMBER

Length: 6 to 18 in (15 to 45 cm)

Range: Tropical and subtropical Atlantic Ocean

Habitat: Seafloor from 0 to 180 ft (55 m)

Diet: Waste materials on the seafloor

Conservation: Not at risk

Chocolate chip sea cucumber

With spikes up to 10 cm (4 in) long, the slate pencil sea urchin lives on coral reefs in the Indian and Pacific Oceans.

The slate pencil can crawl as much as 3.3 ft (1 m) per day in search of algae to eat.

On the underside of the urchin's body is its mouth, armed with teeth for scraping and biting.

DID YOU KNOW? The longest sea cucumber is the tiger tail, which lives on coral reefs in the Atlantic Ocean and reaches 6.6 ft (2 m) long.

Worms

We call invertebrates "worms" when they have a long body and no limbs. Although worms share this basic shape, they belong to several different groups that are not closely related to each other, including flatworms, ribbon worms, and annelid worms, which have bodies divided into segments.

Sessile Worms

Sessile means "fixed in one place." Sessile worms attach themselves to the seafloor, rock, or coral, then build a hard tube around their soft body. Most of them build this tube from a tough mineral that they make in their own body, but some make tubes from mud or sand.

The Christmas tree worm is a sessile annelid worm. It extends two spiral mouthparts from its mineral tube. These mouthparts are covered in feathery tentacles for trapping bits of food.

Bristleworms

There are around 10,000 species of bristleworms, which are annelids. Many bristleworms crawl over the seabed, but some are burrowers, swimmers, or sessile. A few live on land or inside other creatures. Each of a bristleworm's body segments has a pair of paddle-like parapodia (meaning "beside feet"), which are used for movement. The parapodia are covered in bristles, which—in some species—can give a venomous sting.

A species of bristleworm, the bearded fireworm feeds on corals, anemones, and small crustaceans.

As tiny living things float past, the feathery tentacles catch them, sending the food down grooves to the central mouth.

This sessile worm's tube is built from sand and mud stuck together with the worm's own mucus.

BOBBIT WORM

Length: 1.6 to 10 ft (0.5 to 3 m)

Range: Tropical and subtropical Atlantic, Indian, and Pacific Oceans

Habitat: Gravel, mud, or coral seafloor between 30 and 130 ft (10 and 40 m)

Diet: Small fish, invertebrates, and seaweed

Conservation: Not at risk

The Bobbit worm buries itself while waiting for prey.

DID YOU KNOW? If part of the banded nemertean ribbon worm is broken off, it grows into a new worm—200,000 worms can grow from one adult.

Hunter Sharks

Sharks have skeletons made of bendy, lightweight cartilage rather than bone. Their mouths have several rows of teeth. These rows constantly move forward, then fall out and are replaced by the next. Most sharks are hunters, using their teeth for grabbing, biting, or crushing prey.

Shark Senses

Sharks have excellent senses of smell, sight, and hearing. Like most fish, sharks also have a sense system called the lateral line, which uses hairlike cells to feel water movements. In addition, sharks and other cartilaginous fish have sensing organs called ampullae of Lorenzini, which are jelly-filled pores in the skin. These detect electric fields, which are created by all living things when moving their muscles. A shark's ampullae can detect the beating heart of a completely still animal.

Growing up to 20 ft (6.1 m) long and reaching speeds of 35 mph (56 km/h), the great white shark is a fearsome predator. This adult is swallowing a whole seal.

Eye Protection

Many sharks have an extra, see-through eyelid called a nictitating membrane, which they close to protect their eyes when striking prey or being attacked. Some species, such as great white sharks, do not have a nictitating membrane, so they roll their eyeballs backward when lunging at prey.

This Caribbean reef shark has closed its nictitating membrane while holding a struggling lionfish.

SAND TIGER

Length: 6.6 to 10.5 ft (2 to 3.2 m)

Range: Subtropical and temperate Atlantic, Indian, and Pacific Oceans

Habitat: Coastal waters to depths of 620 ft (190 m)

Diet: Bony fish, rays, skates, and smaller sharks, such as smooth-hounds

Conservation: Population shrinking due to fishing

Sand tiger

As in other sharks, the hammerhead's gill slits are not covered. The slits are where water exits the body, after oxygen has been taken from it.

The scalloped hammerhead shark has eyes at either side of its hammer-shaped head. This means the shark can see 360 degrees, above and below.

This shark usually hunts fish such as sardines and mackerel.

DID YOU KNOW? When chasing prey, the shortfin mako shark can swim at up to 42 mph (68 km/h) and leap up to 30 ft (9 m) out of the water.

Filter Feeder Sharks

Three species of sharks use a different method of feeding from their fierce relatives. Whale, megamouth, and basking sharks are filter feeders, straining tiny zooplankton and fish from the water. Although these sharks have hundreds of small teeth, they do not use them for eating.

Big Mouths

Filter feeding sharks have huge mouths. The largest of all is the whale shark's, which is 4.9 ft (1.5 m) wide. Filter feeders have two methods: Either swimming forward with their mouth wide open so that water rushes inside, or sucking in mouthfuls of water. As the water flows out of the back of the mouth through the gills, filter pads in the gills act like sieves, catching tiny animals in the water.

Whale shark skin, which is up to 4 in (10 cm) thick, is marked with pale spots.

Whale sharks feed on small fish, squid, and zooplankton such as krill, eggs, and larvae.

The megamouth shark is so rare that no one knew it existed until 1976. Reaching 18 ft (5.5 m), it is the smallest of the filter feeding sharks.

WHALE SHARK

Length: 18 to 41.5 ft (5.5 to 12.65 m)

Range: Tropical and subtropical Atlantic, Indian, and Pacific Oceans

Habitat: Open ocean to depths of 5,900 ft (1,800 m)

Diet: Zooplankton, small fish, and squid

Conservation: Endangered due to fishing and collisions with boats

Whale shark

DID YOU KNOW? Weighing up to 47,000 lb (21,300 kg), the whale shark is not just the largest fish but the largest animal that is not a mammal.

In one hour, a whale shark can filter more than 21,000 ft³ (600 m³) of water, swallowing 4 to 7 lb (2 to 3 kg) of food.

Threatened Sharks

Of the 440 species of sharks, over 70 are threatened with extinction, including whale and basking sharks. Every year, up to 100 million sharks are killed by fishermen, for food or sport. Most sharks give birth to a small number of live young, rather than releasing lots of eggs like many other fish. As a result, some shark species cannot reproduce fast enough to keep up their numbers.

The second largest species of shark, the basking shark is now protected by law in many countries.

Rays and Relatives

Rays—including skates, guitarfish, and sawfish—make up a group of fish called batoids. Like sharks, batoids have skeletons made of cartilage. They are flat bodied, and many species have extra-large, often wing-like, pectoral fins.

Flapping or Waving

Most batoids swim by moving their pectoral fins. This makes them different from sharks and most other fish, which power through the water using movements of their tail or body. Batoids such as manta rays and eagle rays have wide, pointed pectoral fins that they flap up and down, almost like birds. Batoids with rounder pectoral fins, such as electric rays, wave their fins, with the ruffling wave traveling along the length of each fin.

The largest spotted eagle rays grow up to 16 ft (5 m) long, with a wingspan of up to 10 ft (3 m).

Electric Rays

The 69 species of electric rays make electricity in special organs on either side of their head. All living things, even humans, make tiny amounts of electricity as the body carries out its work, but electric rays make larger amounts and then store it, like in a battery. These rays release a pulse of electricity to kill or stun prey, as well as for defense.

The leopard torpedo ray is a species of electric ray that uses electricity to capture fish, worms, and crustaceans.

Manta rays often visit "cleaning stations," where they pick up angelfish to eat the irritating parasites living on their body.

The cephalic fins channel water into the ray's open mouth, so it can filter feed on zooplankton.

BROWN GUITARFISH

Length: 31 to 39 in (80 to 100 cm)

Range: Tropical and subtropical coasts of the western Pacific Ocean

Habitat: Sandy and muddy seabeds to depths of 750 ft (230 m)

Diet: Fish, shrimp, and squid

Conservation: Not known

Brown guitarfish

DID YOU KNOW? The largest species of electric rays make electric pulses of up to 220 volts, creating a deadly shock similar to dropping a hairdryer into water.

Flatfish

Like most fish, flatfish have skeletons made of bone. They live on the seafloor of all oceans, from the Arctic to the shores of Antarctica. With their flattened body, they are able to lie on their side as they wait—motionless—for passing prey.

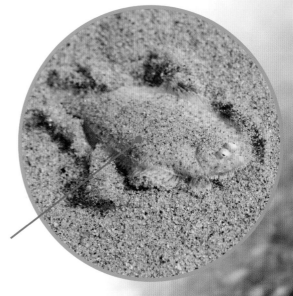

The wide-eyed flounder has both eyes on its left side. Like other flatfish, it can stick up its eyes to get a better view.

Camouflage

Many flatfish are well camouflaged on the seafloor. Although their underside (which may be the left or right side) is pale, their upperside is usually dappled or spotted, to match the seabed. Some flatfish, such as flounder, can change their skin color, releasing pigments to make darker or lighter, smaller or bigger, spots.

This sole is burying itself in sand for extra camouflage. At night, it feeds on worms, mollusks, and small crustaceans.

Moving Eyes

When flatfish hatch from their eggs, they are symmetrical, with one eye on each side of their body. At this stage, they drift through the water rather than living on the bottom. As flatfish grow into adults, one of their eyes moves to the other side of the head. Then the flatfish sinks to the bottom, laying its eyeless side on the floor.

Depending on the species, flatfish have their left or right side uppermost. The European plaice has its right side uppermost.

DID YOU KNOW? Peacock flounders change color to suit their surroundings in 8 seconds, unless one of their eyes is covered by sand, which prevents them color matching.

TURBOT

Length: 16 to 39 in (40 to 100 cm)

Range: European coasts of the northern Atlantic Ocean

Habitat: Sandy or rocky seabeds at depths of 65 to 230 ft (20 to 70 m)

Diet: Fish, crustaceans, and bivalves

Conservation: Population shrinking

Turbot

This flounder is waiting to ambush fish and shrimp.

The dorsal fin extends right round the head. Flatfish belong to the subclass of ray-finned fish, so their fins are supported by bony spines called rays.

Seahorses

These small fish are not covered in scales but in bony plates of armor. This makes them unable to wiggle their bodies to swim, so they flutter their fins to move along slowly. In fact, seahorses are such bad swimmers that they usually remain still, using their curling tail to grip seaweed or coral.

Fathers Giving Birth

Seahorses have a unique method of giving birth. Before mating, a male and female seahorse court each other, dancing snout to snout and holding tails. When she is ready, the female seahorse puts 50 to 1,500 eggs into a pouch on the male's front. The male carries the eggs until they hatch, then releases the tiny young, called fry, into the water.

This male dwarf seahorse is releasing his fry into the water.

The seahorse sucks up microorganisms and tiny crustaceans through its toothless snout.

Barbigant's pygmy seahorse

BARBIGANT'S PYGMY SEAHORSE

Length: 0.5 to 1 in (1.3 to 2.6 cm)

Range: Tropical coasts of the eastern Indian and western Pacific Oceans

Habitat: Sea fan corals at depths of 33 to 130 ft (10 to 40 m)

Diet: Tiny crustaceans

Conservation: Small population, which may need future protection

DID YOU KNOW? The world's slowest-moving fish is the dwarf seahorse, which has a top speed of only 5 ft (1.5 m) per hour.

Seadragons

The three species of seadragons belong to the same family as seahorses. They also have body armor and long snouts for sucking up food. Unlike seahorses, which are among the few fish to swim upright, seadragons swim horizontally and do not have a curling tail. Male seadragons also take care of their eggs, but they carry them on their tail rather than in a pouch.

Seadragons are known for their extraordinary camouflage. The leafy seadragon is covered in leaf-like fronds, which make it look like floating seaweed.

A seahorse's bony plates are arranged in rings down its body. This armor makes a seahorse tricky for predators to bite.

Boxfish and Relatives

The horned boxfish, also called the longhorn cowfish, lives on coral reefs.

Boxfish, sunfish, porcupinefish, pufferfish, and triggerfish all belong to an order of bony fish called Tetraodontiformes (meaning "four teeth" in ancient Greek). Their unusual jaws form a beak shape, with tooth-like bones that are often used for crushing hard-shelled invertebrates.

Strange Bodies

For protection, most fish in this order are covered in bony plates, sharp spines, or tough skin. Their bodies are rigid, so they do not wriggle to swim. Instead, they move by waving their fins. These fish are also known for their strange body shapes, which may be nearly square (boxfish), round (porcupinefish), or flattened (sunfish and triggerfish).

A sunfish has perhaps the strangest-looking body of all fish. It ends behind the dorsal and anal fins, making the fish look as if it has lost its back half.

Puffing Up

Porcupinefish and pufferfish have a very effective defense when they are threatened by predators. They fill their stretchy stomachs with water, puffing the fish up until they are too big for most predators to swallow. In addition, they are covered by sharp spines. If this were not enough, pufferfish and some porcupinefish are also extremely poisonous.

The yellowspotted burrfish is a poisonous species of porcupinefish that lives on coral reefs. It can inflate (right) to nearly twice its normal size (left).

76

CLOWN TRIGGERFISH

Length: 16 to 20 in (40 to 50 cm)

Range: Tropical and subtropical coasts of the Indian and Pacific Oceans

Habitat: Coral reefs to depths of 250 ft (75 m)

Diet: Mollusks, crustaceans, and sea urchins

Conservation: Not known

Clown triggerfish

The tough horns make this fish harder to swallow. When threatened, the boxfish also releases poisonous mucus through its skin.

This boxfish eats algae, worms, crustaceans, and mollusks.

DID YOU KNOW? The ocean sunfish is the heaviest bony fish, weighing up to 5,000 lb (2,300 kg) and reaching 10.8 ft (3.3 m) long.

Surgeonfish and Relatives

Surgeonfish, tangs, and unicornfish usually live on coral reefs. On either side of their body, at the base of their tail, these fish have sharp spines like surgeon's knives. While some species have fixed spines, others have hinged spines that can be flicked out, with a twist of the tail, to wound predators.

Safety in Numbers

Fish in this family feed on algae that grows on coral reefs, grazing on it with their sharp teeth. Patches of algae are often guarded by aggressive damselfish. For this reason, surgeonfish and their relatives often feed in shoals, or groups, which offer defense against damselfish, as well as predators such as tuna and grouper.

These powder blue tangs are shoaling for safety. When the fish in a shoal are all swimming in the same direction, it is called schooling.

ORANGESPOT SURGEONFISH

Length: 8 to 14 in (20 to 35 cm)

Range: Tropical coasts of the eastern Indian and western Pacific Oceans

Habitat: Coral reefs to depths of 260 ft (80 m)

Diet: Algae and diatoms

Conservation: Not at risk

Orangespot surgeonfish

Growing up to 16 in (40 cm) long, the sohal surgeonfish lives on coral reefs in the Red Sea.

Surgeonfish play an important role on coral reefs, as they feed on algae, preventing overgrowth from damaging the coral.

This spine is normally folded against the body, pointing toward the head. When threatened, the fish flicks out the blade.

Unicornfish

As most unicornfish reach adulthood, they grow a bony, horn-like spike between their eyes. Males grow bigger horns than females. Scientists are not sure what use the horn has, since the fish do not use it for fighting, as is the case with horned mammals. It is likely the growth of the horn signals that a fish is big enough for mating.

The bluespine unicornfish has two fixed blue spines at either side of its tail.

DID YOU KNOW? The spines of the lined surgeonfish are venomous, causing painful wounds to humans and death to smaller predators.

Scorpionfish

Many of the world's most venomous species of fish are scorpionfish. These fish inject predators with venom by a prick from their sharp spines, which contain venom-making glands. Most species of scorpionfish live on or near the bottom of the world's warmer oceans.

Sucking Up

Scorpionfish capture prey using a method called suction feeding. Some scorpionfish lie in wait for prey while others hunt for it, but when prey comes close, they all behave the same way. In a fraction of a second, the scorpionfish opens its mouth and expands its cheeks. Water (and the prey in the water) rushes into the scorpionfish's mouth to fill the space.

The 13 long spines of the dorsal fin contain venom glands. There is also one venomous spine in each of the two pelvic fins and three in the anal fin, making 18 in total.

Reef Stonefish

The most venomous fish of all is the reef stonefish, which lives on coral reefs of the tropical Indian and Pacific Oceans. A prick from its spines can be deadly to humans, but luckily there is an antivenom available. What makes this fish dangerous to humans is its habit of sitting on the seafloor, looking just like a rock, as it waits for prey to ambush.

The well-camouflaged tasseled scorpionfish lies in wait for passing fish and crustaceans.

A member of the scorpionfish family, the common lionfish hunts at night for small fish and crustaceans.

The reef stonefish is camouflaged to look like an algae-covered rock (right). Using its pectoral fins as spades, it can bury itself in sand to become even less visible (above right).

SHORTFIN DWARF LIONFISH

Length: 5 to 7 in (12 to 17 cm)

Range: Tropical coasts of the Indian and western Pacific Oceans

Habitat: Coral reefs to depths of 260 ft (80 m)

Diet: Small crustaceans

Conservation: Not at risk

Shortfin dwarf lionfish

The fanlike pectoral fins are not venomous.

DID YOU KNOW? Lionfish are aposematic (from the ancient Greek for "away" and "sign"), which means their bold patterns warn predators that they are dangerous to eat.

Dragonets

These small fish live mainly in the tropical waters of the Indian and Pacific Oceans. Dragonets are usually colorful and highly patterned, with large fins. These features are useful for attracting a mate. Dragonets stay close to sandy seafloors, where they bury themselves to escape predators.

Courting

Before mating, male and female dragonets court each other. During courtship, the two fish spread and display their fins. Then the pair swim upward side by side, rubbing against each other. Finally, near the water surface, the female releases her eggs and the male releases his sperm into the water. The fertilized eggs float away.

Like all dragonets, mandarin dragonets are sexually dimorphic, which means that males and females look different from each other. The male (on the left) is bigger, has longer fins, and is differently patterned.

Fighting

Male dragonets are very aggressive to one another. They most often fight over the right to mate with females, but sometimes they just fight to show their greater strength. During fights, the males chase, wrestle, and bite. Quite often, fights end in the death of the weaker male.

These two male painted dragonets are battling head to head. This species lives only around the coasts of Australia.

The picturesque dragonet's bright patterns help with camouflage in its coral reef habitat.

STARRY DRAGONET

Length: 2 to 3 in (5 to 7.5 cm)

Range: Tropical coasts of the Indian and western Pacific Oceans

Habitat: Coral reefs at depths of 16 to 130 ft (5 to 40 m)

Diet: Small crustaceans, worms, and microorganisms

Conservation: Not known

Starry dragonet

Dragonets have large eyes, positioned on the top of their head. When the dragonet buries itself in sand for defense, its eyes stay uncovered to keep watch.

Dragonets do not have scales, so their skin is protected by a coating of thick, slimy mucus.

DID YOU KNOW? The mandarin dragonet got its name from its colorful pattern, which is like the robes worn by "mandarin" officials who worked for the emperor of China.

Billfish

These large bony fish are fierce predators. They have long bills, or beaks, which are extensions of their upper jaw bones. The bills are used for slashing at prey—and occasionally for spearing it. Billfish include sailfish, marlins, and swordfish.

Fastest Fish

Billfish usually live in the open ocean, far from land. Their long, streamlined bodies and powerful muscles make them excellent swimmers. They travel vast distances in search of food and suitable water temperatures. When pursuing prey, billfish are the fastest fish in the ocean. Scientists do not agree which billfish is the fastest of all: Some say it is the Indo-Pacific sailfish, while others name the black marlin, which has been recorded at 65 mph (105 km/h).

The Atlantic sailfish has a large, sail-like first dorsal fin, which it folds down while swimming. When attacking prey, it raises the sail to steady its side-to-side movement.

Found in the tropical and subtropical Indian and Pacific Oceans, the black marlin can grow to 15.3 ft (4.65 m) long.

Swordfish

The swordfish has the longest bill of all billfish, reaching 1.5 m (4.9 ft). While the bills of other billfish are rounder and more spearlike, the swordfish's is sword-shaped. It is flat, smooth, and sharp. Although some billfish have been known to spear prey, as well as predators such as great white sharks, swordfish use their bills only for slashing.

The swordfish hunts alone, chasing smaller fish such as mackerel and herring, as well as descending to find crustaceans and squid in the darker waters below.

DID YOU KNOW? The biggest billfish is the Indo-Pacific blue marlin, which reaches 16.4 ft (5 m) long and 1,378 lb (625 kg).

The sailfish slashes left to right with its jagged-edged bill, wounding fish to make them easier to catch.

This sailfish is attacking a shoal of sardines from behind, hoping to capture the slowest fish.

WHITE MARLIN

Length: 4.3 to 9.2 ft (1.3 to 2.8 m)

Range: Tropical and subtropical Atlantic Ocean

Habitat: Open ocean to depths of 330 ft (100 m)

Diet: Fish such as flying fish and tuna, as well as squid

Conservation: Population at risk from sport fishing and accidental capture in nets

White marlin

Baleen Whales

Along with dolphins and porpoises, whales belong to the group of marine mammals called cetaceans. Cetaceans power through the water with their tail, steering with their two flippers. They spend their whole life in the water, but surface to breathe air through the blowholes on top of their head. There are 15 species of baleen whales.

Baleen

Baleen whales are named for the plates of bristly baleen in their mouth. Baleen is made of keratin, the same tough material that makes human nails. When they feed, baleen whales take in a mouthful of water, either by lunge-feeding (taking a huge gulp) or skim-feeding (swimming with an open mouth). The water is then released through the baleen plates, which trap small prey inside the mouth.

This gray whale is showing its baleen plates. Gray whales are skim-feeders, scooping up sand, water, and tiny crustaceans as they swim over the seafloor. They live for up to 70 years.

Whale Song

All whales make sounds to communicate with each other. During mating season, male baleen whales are known for their "songs" to attract females. Songs are made up of moans, chirps, and roars. Humpback whales have the most complex songs, lasting 10 to 20 minutes, which are repeated for hours. During each mating season, all humpback males in one region sing the same song, which changes from one season to the next. Sometimes, males in one region copy songs from other regions.

Humpback whales often move in small groups called pods, containing mothers and their calves, but they gather in larger groups during mating season.

SOUTHERN RIGHT WHALE

Length: 36 to 59 ft (11 to 18 m)

Range: Southern Ocean in southern summer; southern Atlantic, Indian, and Pacific Oceans in winter

Habitat: Open ocean in summer; coastlines in winter

Diet: Zooplankton and krill

Conservation: Population stable after huge losses due to hunting in previous centuries

Southern right whale

Barnacles often attach themselves to a humpback whale's skin.

The humpback whale, which reaches 52 ft (16 m) long, often leaps partway out of the water, called breaching.

The flippers have knobbles called tubercles. These are enlarged hair follicles, or roots from which hairs grow.

DID YOU KNOW? The largest animal that ever lived, the blue whale can hold 23,775 gallons (90,000 liters) in its mouth, but cannot swallow anything bigger than a beach ball.

Toothed Whales

Sperm whales, beaked whales, and white whales all have teeth for catching prey, rather than baleen plates. While baleen whales have two blowholes, toothed whales have just one. Scientists also put dolphins and porpoises in the toothed whale group, but those cetaceans are usually smaller.

Echolocation

Sound travels fast and far underwater, unlike light, which does not reach far below the surface. With a method called echolocation, toothed whales use sound to navigate and find prey. They make clicking noises, which travel outward from the whale. The clicks bounce off objects and return. The speed and quality of the returning echoes enable toothed whales to build up a "picture" of their surroundings.

Like the other 22 species of beaked whales, Cuvier's beaked whale uses echolocation to dive deep for squid and fish. Its long jaw bones make a "beak," while the single blowhole is on top of its head.

White Whales

The beluga whale and narwhal (see pages 40–41) make up the family of white whales, which are found in and around the Arctic Ocean. Both these whales are quite small, reaching around 16 ft (5 m) long. They have bulbous heads, creating a "melon" on their forehead. Unlike most whales, they do not have a dorsal fin to help with steering.

The beluga whale dives in search of fish. Since its teeth are small and quite blunt, it has to swallow prey whole.

The sperm whale's squarish head often has scars from teeth scrapes made during battles with other whales.

As in all cetaceans, the tail, called the fluke, is horizontally flattened so it can beat up and down.

The sperm whale dives as deep as 7,380 ft (2,250 m) in search of giant squid.

Sperm whale breaching

SPERM WHALE

Length: 36 to 67 ft (11 to 20.5 m)

Range: All oceans except Arctic and Southern Oceans where covered by ice

Habitat: Usually deep oceans away from coasts

Diet: Squid, sharks, rays, and other large fish

Conservation: Threatened by tangling in nets, collisions with boats, global warming, pollution, and ocean noise

DID YOU KNOW? A Cuvier's beaked whale holds the record for the longest underwater dive by a mammal: 137 minutes.

Dolphins

Dolphins are small toothed whales, with a streamlined body for fast swimming and cone-shaped teeth for grasping prey. Dolphins make a wide range of sounds to communicate with each other, from clicks to whistles. Around 30 species of dolphins live in the oceans, with another 4 species living in rivers.

Living in a Pod

Dolphins are very sociable, living in pods that differ in size from species to species. A small pod may contain just a mother and her calves. Sometimes, family groups join together to number over a hundred dolphins—or even thousands where there is plenty of prey. Dolphins show strong bonds between friends and relatives. They often help weaker members of their pod, staying beside injured friends or helping them to the surface to breathe.

Up to 26 ft (8 m) long, orcas are the largest dolphins, but are sometimes called killer whales. Pods are led by the oldest female and contain her children and their children.

Acrobatics

Dolphins often leap above the water surface. Sometimes this is the quickest way of traveling, as it is easier to move through air than water. At other times, dolphins leap to see what is going on, to show off to each other, to shake parasites off their skin—or just to play. Dolphins sometimes play in other ways, by chasing each other or by tossing around objects.

Spinner dolphins are named for their habit of spinning around as they leap through the air.

Common bottlenose dolphins are 6.6 to 13 ft (2 to 4 m) long and live for 40 to 50 years.

This dolphin gets its name from its beak, which looks a little like the neck of a bottle.

Common bottlenose dolphins live in pods of around 15, often working together to capture shoals of fish.

STRIPED DOLPHIN

Length: 6.6 to 7.9 ft (2 to 2.4 m)

Range: Temperate to tropical Atlantic, Indian, and Pacific Oceans

Habitat: Usually deep oceans away from coasts

Diet: Fish, squid, octopus, krill, and other crustaceans

Conservation: Population shrinking due to tangling in nets, collisions with boats, and pollution

Striped dolphins

DID YOU KNOW? The smallest dolphin is the critically endangered Maui's dolphin, which lives off the coast of New Zealand and reaches 5.6 ft (1.7 m) long.

Porpoises

Porpoises are closely related to dolphins, but they do not have beaks and have spade-shaped rather than cone-shaped teeth. There are seven species of porpoises, including the tiniest cetacean of all, the vaquita, which is just 4.6 ft (1.4 m) long.

Life at Sea

Female porpoises are pregnant for a full year before giving birth to just one calf in the water. Mothers produce milk, which is thick like toothpaste, so it can be squirted into the calf's mouth. The milk is high in fat, which helps the calf develop its thick layer of body fat, called blubber. As in all cetaceans, blubber keeps a porpoise warm, even in deep waters and polar regions.

Porpoises are preyed on by sharks and orcas. This orca is hurling a harbour porpoise through the air to weaken it for capture.

Since the finless porpoise lives in coastal waters, it is particularly at risk from human behavior.

Most Endangered

The finless, narrow-ridged finless, and vaquita porpoises are all at risk of extinction. The vaquita is the most endangered cetacean of all, with only around 10 left in 2019. The vaquita lives in the northern Gulf of California, off the coast of Mexico. Major threats to the vaquita, and all other porpoises, include accidental capture in fishing nets and water pollution.

Conservationists are working hard to save the last vaquitas. Even photos of this critically endangered cetacean are extremely rare.

DID YOU KNOW? Porpoises sleep with one eye and half their brain at a time, while the other side controls the blowhole and stays partly alert—then the porpoise swaps sides.

DALL'S PORPOISE

Length: 5.9 to 7.5 ft (1.8 to 2.3 m)

Range: Temperate and subarctic northern Pacific Ocean

Habitat: Usually deep oceans away from coasts

Diet: Fish, squid, and crustaceans

Conservation: Population at risk in some areas from hunting

Dall's porpoise

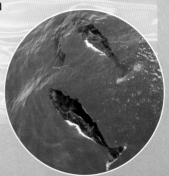

Found along coasts in the northern hemisphere, the harbour porpoise has a small, rounded head with no beak.

Porpoises have large pupils, enabling plenty of light to enter the eye and giving good vision while diving deep for fish and squid.

The harbour porpoise's dorsal fin is almost triangular, helping the cetacean to steer.

Sea Cows

The sea cows, also called sirenians, are an order of mammals that live in warm and shallow water, ranging from coastal seas to swamps and rivers. They are mostly plant-eaters, using their strong lips to rip off leaves and stems. They have heavy bones and rounded bodies, making them slow swimmers.

The West Indian manatee lives on the warm eastern coast of the Americas, from the United States to Brazil, often swimming inland up rivers.

The Dugong

The dugong, which reaches 10 ft (3 m) long and lives for up to 70 years, is one of the four species of sea cows. It lives in warm coastal waters of the Indian and Pacific Oceans. Like all sea cows, it has no dorsal fin or back limbs, but has flipper-like front limbs. Unlike its relatives, the manatees, its snout is downturned, which makes it easier to feed on bottom-growing seagrass. It has peglike teeth for grinding plants.

The dugong's two nostrils are closed by valves when it is underwater. It can last up to six minutes before going to the water surface to breathe.

This West Indian manatee calf is drinking milk from its mother. Her teats are just behind her flippers. Mothers and calves squeak to communicate with each other.

Manatees

There are three species of manatees. The West Indian and African manatees live both in coastal waters and nearby rivers and wetlands. The Amazonian manatee lives only in the Amazon River, in South America. Manatees usually swim alone, apart from mothers and their calves, which stay together for up to 18 months. Adults also form groups in the mating season.

Like all mammals, the manatee has body hair. The manatee's hairs are extremely sensitive, enabling it to feel slight movements in the murky water.

The manatee's tail is flattened and paddle-like.

AFRICAN MANATEE

Length: 9.8 to 14.8 ft (3 to 4.5 m)

Range: Tropical coasts of western Africa

Habitat: Shallow coastal ocean, rivers, and lakes

Diet: Mostly plants, including mangrove leaves and seagrass, as well as bivalves

Conservation: Population shrinking due to hunting and habitat loss

African manatee

DID YOU KNOW? The closest living relatives of sea cows are elephants, which are also plant-eating mammals with thick skin.

Polar Bear

The polar bear lives on and around the Arctic Ocean, where it hunts for its favorite food: seals. These bears are born on land, but spend most of their life on the ice that covers the ocean surface, sometimes diving into the cold water. They have thick body fat and fur to keep them warm.

Born in a Den

During the fall when a female polar bear is pregnant, she digs a den in the snow, then climbs inside to rest. Snow soon covers the entrance, making it warm inside. Usually, the mother gives birth to two cubs, which start out completely blind. Although the mother has not eaten since entering her den, she feeds the cubs on her milk. In the spring, the family finally leaves the den and heads for the sea ice, where the mother hunts for prey for them all.

Cubs stay with their mother until they are about two and a half years old.

Hunting Seals

Polar bears usually catch seals when they come to holes in the ice to breathe. Bears use their powerful sense of smell to find a seal breathing hole, then crouch to wait. When a seal pops up, the bear drags it out with a clawed paw. Sometimes, polar bears creep close to seals that are resting on the ice, rushing forward in a final deadly attack.

Polar bears eat as many seals as possible from winter to summer, storing up energy for the late summer and fall, when the sea ice melts and hunting is difficult.

DID YOU KNOW? The longest known underwater dive by a polar bear lasted 3 minutes and 10 seconds.

The bear can smell a seal at a distance of 1 mile (1.6 km).

The paws are large to help with swimming and to spread the bear's weight so it does not sink into snow or crash through thin sea ice.

A polar bear's coat appears white, but its hairs are actually colourless and see-through.

POLAR BEAR

Length: 5.9 to 9.8 ft (1.8 to 3 m)

Range: The coastal Arctic Ocean and surrounding land

Habitat: Sea ice, ocean, and land when sea ice melts in late summer to fall

Diet: Ringed, bearded, and other seals, plus bird eggs and dead walruses and whales

Conservation: Population at risk from global warming

Polar bear

Otters

There are 13 species of otters, which are meat-eating mammals that spend part or most of their lives in either saltwater or freshwater. Two species, the sea and marine otters, live only in saltwater, while the Eurasian otter moves between coastal oceans and rivers. All the other otters live around freshwater.

Sea Otter

Unlike other marine mammals, otters do not have blubber, so their slim bodies are covered in thick fur to keep them warm. The sea otter lives in coastal waters of the northern and eastern Pacific Ocean. Its back paws are wide and webbed for paddling, while the smaller front paws have sharp claws for catching prey. The sea otter dives to the seafloor in search of sea urchins, mollusks, crustaceans, and fish. This clever otter is known for using rocks to break open tough shells.

This sea otter is cracking open a clam on the side of a boat.

Sea otters sleep and rest together in large single-sex groups called rafts, sometimes holding each other's paws.

EURASIAN OTTER

Length: 3 to 4.6 ft (0.9 to 1.4 m)

Range: Rivers and coasts of Europe, North Africa, and Asia

Habitat: Rivers, lakes, and coastal oceans with freshwater nearby for washing off salt

Diet: Fish, crustaceans, insects, and birds

Conservation: Population shrinking in some regions due to habitat loss and pollution

Eurasian otter

To stop themselves from drifting out to sea while sleeping, the otters wrap themselves in kelp.

Sea otters float easily on their back, helped by air trapped in their fur.

Marine Otter

Unlike the sea otter, which spends nearly all its life in the ocean, the marine otter spends a lot of time on rocky beaches. It is found along the western coast of South America, where it hunts for crabs, mollusks, shrimps, and fish. Like the sea otter, the marine otter is endangered by oil spills and other pollution. In the past, it was hunted for its fur.

The marine otter's muscular tail helps with steering through the water.

DID YOU KNOW? The sea otter has the thickest fur of any animal, with up to 1 million per square inch (150,000 hairs per square cm).

Walrus

Although it is closely related to seals, the walrus is the only species in its family. The walrus has four flippers, long tusks, and whiskers. Its thick blubber makes it extremely heavy, sometimes weighing as much as 4,400 lb (2,000 kg), and keeps it warm in the freezing temperatures of the far north.

Whiskers

Walruses have mats of bristly whiskers, called vibrissae, on their snout. These hairs are linked to nerves, making them extremely sensitive. Walruses use their whiskers for feeling movement in the water and for finding prey on the muddy, dark seabed.

This walrus calf (left) and its mother (right) have 400 to 700 whiskers. The calf will stay with its mother for up to five years.

Tusks

Both male and female walruses have tusks, but a male's tusks are slightly longer, reaching up to 3.3 ft (1 m). Tusks are the walrus's canine teeth, which are the pointed, fanglike teeth in all mammals. Tusks are used for making breathing holes in the sea ice from the water below, and for help with climbing out onto slippery ice. Male walruses also use their tusks for fighting, to keep other males away from their mates.

Outside the mating season, hundreds of walruses crowd together in single-sex groups on beaches.

During mating season, male walruses often fight in the water. The largest males with the biggest tusks usually win.

These males are sunbathing, heating up before or after dives into the cold water. Their warming blood makes their skin look pink.

Walrus skin is between 0.8 and 4 in (2 and 10 cm) thick and covered in sparse hair.

Walrus

WALRUS

Length: 7.2 to 11.8 ft (2.2 to 3.6 m)

Range: Coastal Arctic Ocean and far northern Atlantic and Pacific Oceans

Habitat: Sea ice, shallow coastal ocean, and rocky beaches

Diet: Clams and other bivalves, worms, shrimp, and crabs

Conservation: Population at risk from global warming and hunting

DID YOU KNOW? Due to its great size, the walrus has only two non-human predators—polar bears and orcas—but sometimes defends itself successfully against both.

Seals

There are 18 species of true seals. They have a streamlined body suited to swimming and deep diving, with two large back flippers for paddling and two smaller, clawed front flippers for steering. Since their back flippers cannot be pulled under the body for walking, true seals have to wriggle along on land.

Living for up to 35 years, the harbor seal is found in coastal waters of the northern Atlantic and Pacific Oceans.

Fast Parenting

True seals are so well suited to life in the ocean that they rarely go ashore. However, they do come to land, or onto sea ice, to give birth. A mother gives birth to only one pup, which she feeds on extremely high-fat milk for just a few days or weeks, depending on the species. Then the mother must return to the sea to hunt so she can survive. The pup lives off the fat it has built up until it has learned to hunt for itself.

A young Weddell seal yelps to tell its mother it is hungry for milk.

Elephant Seals

The largest seal is the southern elephant seal, with males reaching 19.7 ft (6 m) long. Elephant seals are named for the male's large snout, which looks a little like an elephant's trunk. The hollow, muscly snout acts a bit like a horn, making the male's roars even louder. Elephant seals are able to hold their breath for more than 100 minutes, longer than any mammal that is not a cetacean.

A seal's eyes can see well underwater and in air. When diving, a nictitating membrane, or see-through third eyelid, covers the eyeball for protection.

The male elephant seal roars to warn away other males, who might try to compete for females.

Like other true seals, which are also known as earless seals, the harbor seal has no ear flaps around the openings to its ears.

GRAY SEAL

Length: 5.2 to 10.8 ft (1.6 to 3.3 m)

Range: Coastal northern Atlantic Ocean

Habitat: Coastal ocean, rocks, islands, and beaches

Diet: Fish, octopus, and lobsters

Conservation: Population growing since bans on hunting

Gray seal

DID YOU KNOW? The Weddell seal lives farther south than any other mammal, since it lives on the sea ice surrounding Antarctica.

Eared Seals

Sea lions and fur seals are known as eared seals, because unlike true seals, the opening to their ear is covered by an ear flap. There are six species of sea lions and nine species of fur seals, which are found in all the world's oceans, apart from the Arctic and northern Atlantic Oceans.

Walking on All Fours

Unlike true seals, which have small front paws, eared seals have large front flippers. Their back flippers can also be turned forward, enabling eared seals to walk on all fours. This makes them much more agile when on land, where they spend more of their time than true seals. Large and noisy groups of sea lions or fur seals, called rookeries, can be seen on beaches. Female eared seals spend longer caring for their pups than true seals: Up to a year. When mothers go hunting, pups often gather together to play.

These friendly female California sea lions have gathered underwater, close to their rookery.

The endangered Australian sea lion lives on the beaches and in the coastal waters of southwestern Australia.

NORTHERN FUR SEAL

Length: 4.9 to 6.9 ft (1.5 to 2.1 m)

Range: Coastal northern Pacific Ocean

Habitat: Ocean and beaches

Diet: Fish and squid

Conservation: Population at risk from global warming, pollution, and tangling in nets

Northern fur seal rookery

DID YOU KNOW? Eared seals are known for their loud barking and honking to each other, but also make trumpet sounds when a predator has been spotted.

Female California sea lions are around 5.9 ft (1.8 m) long, while males average 7.9 ft (2.4 m) long.

Hair or Fur

Sea lions have short, rough hair, but fur seals have soft fur. Fur combines coarse "guard" hairs with thicker, softer underfur. During the eighteenth and nineteenth centuries, fur seals were widely hunted for their fur. Some species, including the Cape, northern, and Guadalupe fur seals, were hunted almost to extinction. Since hunting has been banned or limited by many countries, most species have slowly recovered.

When it is wet, the South American fur seal looks almost black, but its fur dries to grey or light brown.

The ear flaps, which direct sounds into the ear, enable the sea lion to hear well both above and below water.

Sea Turtles

From smallest to largest, the seven species of sea turtles are the Kemp's ridley, olive ridley, hawksbill, flatback, green, loggerhead, and leatherback. A sea turtle's large but streamlined body is protected by a shell divided into two parts: covering the back is the carapace, while covering the underside is the plastron.

Nesting on a Beach

At the start of mating season, sea turtles swim from their feeding areas to their coastal mating areas, which may be thousands of miles away. When a female is ready to lay her eggs, she climbs onto the beach, usually at night, and digs a hole in the sand using her back flippers. She lays a clutch of soft-shelled eggs, covers them with smoothed sand to disguise the spot, then returns to the sea. After 50 to 60 days, female babies hatch from eggs that were kept warmer, while males hatch from cooler eggs.

Female loggerhead turtles always nest on the beach where they were born. They lay around 100 eggs in each nest, making about four nests per season. Just a handful of babies will survive to adulthood.

This olive ridley turtle is swimming through plastic rubbish, which it might mistake for food, clogging its stomach.

At Risk

Sea turtles are among the world's most threatened animals. The Kemp's ridley and hawksbill turtles are "critically endangered," while the green turtle is "endangered." The other species, apart from the flatback, are "vulnerable," which means they will become endangered if care is not taken. Threats faced by sea turtles include damage to their nesting beaches, water pollution, tangling in fishing nets, and rising sea temperatures.

FLATBACK TURTLE

Length: 30 to 39 in (76 to 100 cm)

Range: Coastal waters of Australia and New Guinea, in the Indian and Pacific Oceans

Habitat: Tropical and subtropical waters with soft beds, at depths up to 200 ft (60 m)

Diet: Soft coral, shrimp, jellyfish, and sea cucumbers

Conservation: At risk from habitat damage and pollution

A flatback turtle hatchling

The mouth is sharp and hooked, like a beak, which makes it ideal for eating tough sea sponges, algae, and jellyfish.

The carapace is made up of 13 overlapping bony plates called scutes.

Growing to around 45 in (114 cm) long, the hawksbill lives mainly on tropical coral reefs in the Atlantic, Indian, and Pacific Oceans.

DID YOU KNOW? The longest-lived sea turtle is the green turtle, which can survive for more than 80 years in the wild.

Crocodiles and a Lizard

Two species of crocodiles and one species of lizard swim in the oceans. Like most reptiles, they are cold-blooded, which means their body becomes hotter or colder depending on the water and air temperature. These reptiles warm up after swimming by going ashore to bask in the sun.

The Saltwater Crocodile

The saltwater crocodile lives along the coasts of northern Australia and southern Asia. The largest living reptile, with jaws up to 39 in (98 cm) long, this crocodile is an apex predator. Its aggression makes it a threat not only to its common prey—which ranges from sharks to birds and crabs—but also to humans. The crocodile lies in wait, then swims at prey at up to 18 mph (29 km/h). It either drowns its victim, by pulling it underwater, or swallows it whole.

The marine iguana's snout is short, with sharp three-pointed teeth, for scraping algae off rocks.

The saltwater crocodile has one of the strongest bites of any animal, due to its immensely strong, large jaw muscles.

American crocodile

AMERICAN CROCODILE

Length: 8.2 to 19.7 ft (2.5 to 6 m)

Range: Coasts of the Americas, from Florida, USA, to Peru, in the Atlantic and Pacific Oceans

Habitat: Coastal ocean, rivers, lakes, and swamps

Diet: Fish, frogs, turtles, birds, and small mammals

Conservation: Threatened by habitat loss

The iguana has a row of spines along its back.

The Marine Iguana

The marine iguana lives only on the shores of the Galápagos Islands, off the western coast of South America. There are seven or eight slightly different-looking subspecies, which have evolved on the different islands. All of them eat algae. Females and smaller males eat algae exposed on the beach at low tide, or in shallow water. Large males, which reach 140 cm (55 in) long, can dive as deep as 30 m (98 ft) and spend up to 1 hour underwater while feeding.

This marine iguana is grazing on algae on seabed rocks.

Like other lizards, as well as snakes, the marine iguana has skin covered in small, horny scales.

DID YOU KNOW? Saltwater crocodiles have 66 teeth, with the longest ones (the fourth teeth from the front on the lower jaw) up to 3.5 in (9 cm) long.

Plovers and Relatives

Plovers and their relatives are called waders or shorebirds. They often live on beaches and mudflats, where they search for invertebrates in the sand or mud. They are small to medium birds, with long legs for wading through the shallows. Many of them also have long beaks for probing.

The wrybill is a species of plover that lives along the coasts of New Zealand, flying inland to nest beside rivers in spring.

Oystercatchers

Oystercatchers have large orange or red beaks that they use for opening the shells of mollusks such as oysters, mussels, and limpets. These birds usually attack their prey when the tide is going out, before the invertebrates have fully closed their shells after feeding. Oystercatchers also dig in soft sand and mud to find worms.

The Magellanic oystercatcher has yellow eyes, surrounded by a ring of yellow skin.

Black-necked stilt

BLACK-NECKED STILT

Length: 13 to 14 in (34 to 36 cm)

Range: The Americas, from the United States to Argentina

Habitat: Coasts and wetlands

Diet: Small invertebrates, fish, and tadpoles

Conservation: Population shrinking in some regions due to habitat loss

DID YOU KNOW? Plovers get their name from the Latin word "*pluvia*," meaning rain, because people used to think they formed flocks when it was about to rain.

The wrybill's beak bends to the right, making it the only bird in the world with a beak that kinks to one side. The bend helps with reaching invertebrates hiding beneath rocks.

Avocets and Stilts

These waders have long, thin legs and beaks, as well as striking plumage, usually featuring black and white patches. Avocets feed by sweeping their upturned beak from side to side through shallow water or across the surface of mud, as they feel and look for shrimp, insects, and worms. Stilts usually hunt by sight alone, using their straight beak to jab into the water to seize small invertebrates and fish.

These male and female American avocets are courting each other, bowing and swaying from side to side. Soon the pair will build a saucer-shaped nest of twigs close to the water.

Gray and white plumage offers camouflage on stony or sandy shores and riverbeds.

Herons and Relatives

Herons, spoonbills, and the hamerkop are large wading birds with long legs and beaks. They live around the edges of oceans or freshwater. They have four toes, with three pointing forward and one backward. The toes are long, with a little webbing between them, to prevent the birds sinking into mud.

The Goliath Heron

The largest heron, the Goliath stands up to 5 ft (1.5 m) tall and has a wingspan, from wingtip to wingtip, of 7.5 ft (2.3 m). It is found in Africa, around coral reefs, mangrove forests, lakes, and swamps. When hunting, the Goliath usually stands completely still in shallow water. When a fish swims past, the bird spears it with an open beak, then swallows it whole.

The plumage of the Goliath heron's head and neck is chestnut colored.

The feathers' pink shade is gained from eating crustaceans that eat lots of red algae.

DID YOU KNOW? A spoonbill's nostrils are at the base of its beak, close to its eyes, so it can breathe when its beak is underwater during hunting.

The Hamerkop

This African bird hunts for fish, frogs, and shrimp in shallow water. It is found around saltwater, including mangrove forests, as well as freshwater. The only species in its family, the hamerkop is unusual for a wader because it spends a lot of time building giant stick nests in trees, often above water. Nests take up to 14 weeks to construct and can reach 5 ft (1.5 m) across.

Hamerkops build far more nests than they need, up to five per year.

To catch invertebrates, the bird swings its flat and spoon-shaped beak from side to side while wading through shallow water.

Hamerkops often stand on top of one another, perhaps as a way of forming bonds within their flock.

The roseate spoonbill lives around coasts and freshwater in the tropical and subtropical Americas.

TRICOLORED HERON

Length: 22 to 30 in (56 to 76 cm)

Range: Coasts of the Americas, from the northeastern United States to Brazil

Habitat: Mangrove forests, bays, and coastal marshes

Diet: Fish, amphibians, crustaceans, and insects

Conservation: Not at risk

Tricolored heron

Larids

Gulls, skimmers, and skuas are members of the Lari suborder. They are large seabirds that pluck fish from the ocean surface. These bold birds are also known to attack other birds, snatching their food and stealing eggs. Some have adapted to living inland and taking food wherever they find it, including rubbish tips.

Kleptoparasitism

Kleptoparasitism is when an animal eats the food that another animal has caught. Most gulls and skuas steal from other seabirds, either from time to time or, in the case of the great skua, as a main feeding method. The kleptoparasite attacks the other bird—using its own strength, large size, and sharp beak—until it drops its catch. Gulls do not stop at stealing from other birds: Some swoop on humans' food, particularly takeout food eaten on the beach.

A laughing gull is trying to force a white ibis to drop its fish. This gull eats anything it can find, from fish and mollusks to insects, eggs, chicks, and human food waste.

Skimmers

Skimmers have an unusual beak shape, with the lower jaw longer than the upper. This enables them to hunt by flying low over the water, with their beak slightly open. As the beak skims the water surface, the bird snatches up any small fish that are not quick enough to dart away.

Measuring up to 20 in (50 cm) long, the black skimmer hunts in the coastal waters of the Americas, as well as in rivers and lakes.

This gull has a wingspan of up to 4 ft (1.2 m).

The Heermann's gull watches brown pelicans as they hunt, then swoops to steal fish from their throat pouch.

The brown pelican scoops fish and water into its throat pouch. While it drains the water before swallowing, it is at risk from kleptoparasites.

GREAT SKUA

Length: 20 to 23 in (50 to 58 cm)

Range: Northern Atlantic Ocean

Habitat: Open ocean; nests on coasts and islands

Diet: Fish, birds, eggs, mice, rabbits, berries, and dead animals

Conservation: Not at risk

A great skua feeds on an Arctic tern.

DID YOU KNOW? A herring gull was spotted using bits of bread as bait to catch goldfish in a pond in Paris, France.

Tubenoses

Albatrosses, petrels, and shearwaters are tubenoses, named for their beak shape. These seabirds have three webbed toes for paddling in the water, and many have wide wings for flying great distances over the ocean in search of fish. They nest in large groups, called colonies, often on remote islands.

Tube Nostrils

Tubenoses have large tube-shaped nostrils on the top or sides of their beak. These help to give the birds a very good sense of smell, which they use for finding prey and their home colony. In addition, tubenose beaks are covered in horny plates and hooked at the tip. Like other seabirds, tubenoses have a salt gland above their eyes. This gets rid of the salt they take in while swimming and eating. The gland releases salty liquid, which exits through the nostrils and drips down a groove in the beak.

Saltwater is dripping from the beak of this southern giant petrel.

Diving Petrels

Most tubenoses pluck prey from the water surface, but the diving petrels make dives of up to 260 ft (80 m) underwater. Unlike their relatives, diving petrels are small with short wings, so they feed close to shore instead of making long flights. When diving, they half-fold their wings, using them as paddles.

Like other diving petrels, the South Georgia diving petrel flies low over the waves, its feet just touching the surface, making it look like it is walking on water. Petrels are named after St Peter, who was said to walk on water.

DID YOU KNOW? The wandering albatross has the largest wingspan of any bird, reaching 12.1 ft (3.7 m) wide.

WANDERING ALBATROSS

Length: 42 to 53 in (107 to 135 cm)

Range: Southern Ocean and southern Atlantic, Indian, and Pacific Oceans

Habitat: Open ocean; nests on islands

Diet: Squid, fish, crustaceans, and waste from ships

Conservation: Population shrinking due to tangling in fishing lines and pollution

Wandering albatross

The pillar-like nest is built from mud.

The black-browed albatross has smaller nostril tubes, on either side of its beak, than some of its relatives.

Just one egg is laid per year. The chick stays in the nest for around four months.

Gannets and Relatives

Gannets, boobies, cormorants, and frigatebirds are members of the Suliformes order. They are medium to large birds with hooked or cone-shaped beaks. All four of their toes are fully webbed. Apart from frigatebirds, which snatch fish from the water surface, these birds are expert underwater divers.

Found only on the Galápagos Islands, the flightless cormorant has evolved to be such a good swimmer that it has lost the ability to fly.

Diving Styles

Cormorants dive from the water surface, swimming to depths of up to 150 ft (45 m) using their strong, webbed feet. Gannets and boobies are plunge divers, dropping into the water from a height. For this reason, they do not have nostrils on the outside of their beak, which would fill with water as they crashed into the ocean. Instead, they breathe through their mouth. They also have air sacs in their face and chest, which act like cushions.

The northern gannet plunge dives from heights of up to 150 ft (45 m), reaching 62 mph (100 km/h) as it hits the water.

RED-FOOTED BOOBY

Length: 26 to 30 in (65 to 75 cm)

Range: Tropical Atlantic, Indian, and Pacific Oceans

Habitat: Open ocean; nests on islands

Diet: Small fish and squid

Conservation: Not at risk

Red-footed booby

The cormorant propels itself through the water using its large feet and sturdy legs.

The wings are far too small to lift this large bird, up to 3.3 ft (1 m) long, off the ground.

Frigatebirds

There are five species of frigatebirds, which live around tropical and subtropical oceans. During mating season, frigatebirds cluster on remote islands in colonies of up to 5,000 birds. The males of all species have a bright red throat pouch. To attract females, the males inflate their throat pouch, lift their head, and open and shake their wings.

This male great frigatebird is hoping to attract a female.

DID YOU KNOW? "Booby" comes from the Spanish slang word *bobo*, meaning silly, as these birds often landed on sailing ships and were quickly eaten by sailors.

Sea Ducks

Although most people think of ducks as freshwater birds, more than 20 species spend part of their year in coastal seas. Ducks have broad, rounded bodies that float easily at the water surface, webbed feet, and strong legs for paddling.

Diving Ducks

Many freshwater ducks feed by tipping themselves up in shallow water, reaching to the bottom with their tails in the air. These "dabbling" ducks mostly feed on water plants. In contrast, most sea ducks are divers, able to swim to the bottom of deep water to prey on water creatures. Diving ducks usually have bigger feet, set farther back on their body, than dabblers, making them waddle awkwardly on land.

The common eider dives for mussels, which it swallows whole. The shells are crushed in a muscly part of the stomach called the gizzard.

The common scoter spends its winters along the coasts of the northern Atlantic Ocean.

Useful Beaks

Like all birds, ducks do not have teeth, so they swallow their food whole. Their strong beak and jaw enable them to tear off plants or grapple with prey. A duck's beak shape is suited to its diet. Scoter ducks have large, broad beaks for poking in mud and grasping hard-shelled crustaceans and mollusks. The mergansers are fish-eaters, with jagged edges to their long, thin beaks, which helps them grasp their slippery prey.

The red-breasted merganser hunts for small salmon and trout.

This bird is often found on coastal mudflats.

The three front toes are connected by webbing, while the fourth, back toe is very small.

This male common shelduck has a bright red beak, which it uses to dig for mollusks, crustaceans, and insects.

SPECTACLED EIDER

Length: 20 to 22 in (52 to 57 cm)

Range: Arctic and northern Pacific Oceans

Habitat: Open ocean and coastal waters; nests on wetlands

Diet: Mollusks, crustaceans, insects, grasses, and berries

Conservation: Population shrinking due to climate change

Spectacled eider

DID YOU KNOW? In the past, eider ducks were hunted for the layer of very soft, thick "down" feathers next to their skin, which were used to make eiderdowns.

Puffins and Relatives

Puffins are members of the auk family, along with the murres and auklets. These seabirds are high-speed underwater divers, using their wings as paddles. In the air, they have to flap their short wings very quickly to stay aloft. On land, they are clumsy walkers, with an upright penguin-like posture.

Both male and female tufted puffins grow long tufts of feathers as mating season approaches.

Egg Laying

Birds in the auk family spend most of their life far out to sea, but they go ashore during the mating season, when they gather in colonies along the coast. They often return to the same mate year after year, laying just one egg per year. Most species nest on cliff ledges or in rock clefts, where their egg is out of reach from predators.

The thick-billed murre lays its egg on a cliff ledge. The egg is pointed at one end, which means it rolls in a circle rather than off the ledge.

PARAKEET AUKLET

Length: 9 to 10 in (23 to 26 cm)

Range: Northern Pacific Ocean

Habitat: Open ocean; nests on rocky islands

Diet: Jellyfish, crustaceans, and small fish

Conservation: Population shrinking on some islands due to accidental introduction of rats

Parakeet auklet

DID YOU KNOW? By around 1852, the great auk had been driven to extinction by human hunters who wanted its soft feathers, eggs, and meat.

After the mating season ends, the bright red feet will fade.

With short wings but a stocky body, the puffin finds takeoff easiest when it launches into the air from a high cliff.

Deft Divers

Auks need to move fast underwater to capture the quickly swimming fish that are usually their food, including cod, herring, and sandeel. The birds must hold their breath throughout a dive, so they angle their streamlined body to descend to their desired depth as swiftly as possible, then use up and down wing strokes to change direction as they pursue their prey.

The common murre can dive to depths of 590 ft (180 m), never staying underwater for more than 200 seconds.

Penguins

A penguin's small wings, which are shaped like a dolphin's flippers, cannot lift it into the air at all. These seabirds spend three-quarters of their life swimming in the ocean, with most species living in the cold waters of the southern hemisphere. Their blubber and thick, waterproof feathers keep them warm.

Hunters

Penguins dive for fish, squid, and krill. The largest species, such as the 43 in/110 cm-tall emperor penguin, can dive as deep as 1,855 ft (565 m) and stay underwater for up to 22 minutes. Smaller species, such as the little penguin that is only 13 in (33 cm) tall, cannot swim as fast or hold their breath so long, and find their food near the surface. All penguins catch prey in their beak and swallow it whole as they swim.

When the gentoo penguin is swimming, its movements look similar to a bird flying through the air. When the gentoo comes ashore, it is on Antarctica or islands in the far southern seas.

Getting Together

Penguins are sociable birds: They hunt, sleep on the water surface, and nest with other penguins. Many species come to land only to mate, when they gather in large and loud colonies. Penguins often return to the same mate year after year. However, females desert their mate if he no longer seems healthy. A large body size, a deep call, and bright feathers are signs of fitness. In most species, males and females share the exhausting care of their eggs and young chicks.

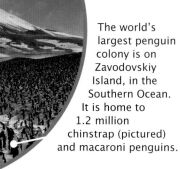

The world's largest penguin colony is on Zavodovskiy Island, in the Southern Ocean. It is home to 1.2 million chinstrap (pictured) and macaroni penguins.

Up to 3.3 ft (1 m) tall, the king penguin gathers to mate on islands in the cold southern oceans.

Parents take turns warming their egg, balancing it on their feet and tucked inside a pouch of skin.

Most penguins lay two eggs, but the king penguin lays only one, which takes 55 days to hatch.

SOUTHERN ROCKHOPPER PENGUIN

Length: 18 to 23 in (45 to 58 cm)

Range: Southern Atlantic, Indian, and Pacific Oceans

Habitat: Open ocean; nests on rocky islands and coasts

Diet: Krill, fish, squid, and octopus

Conservation: Population shrinking due to climate change, overfishing, and oil spills

Southern rockhopper penguin

DID YOU KNOW? The Galápagos penguin is the only penguin that does not live in the southern hemisphere, as its island home straddles the equator.

Glossary

ALGAE
Simple plants and plantlike chromists that usually live in and around water, such as seaweeds.

ANAL FIN
A fin on a fish's underside, toward the tail.

ANTENNA
A slender "feeler" found on the head of some invertebrates.

APPENDAGE
A body part that extends from the body or head, such as an antenna.

ARTHROPOD
An invertebrate with a hard covering, or exoskeleton, and jointed legs, such as an insect or crab.

BACTERIA
Microscopic living things with one simple cell.

BIOLUMINESCENT
Able to make its own light.

BIVALVE
A soft-bodied invertebrate that lives in a hinged two-part shell, such as a clam or mussel.

BLOOD VESSEL
A tube that carries blood through an animal's body.

BLUBBER
A thick layer of fat, found in water-dwelling mammals and penguins, which keeps the animal warm.

CAMOUFLAGE
The way the color and shape of an animal make it less visible in its habitat.

CARTILAGINOUS
With a skeleton made of bendy cartilage rather than bone.

CETACEAN
A water-living mammal with a streamlined body and two flippers; a whale, dolphin, or porpoise.

CHROMIST
A living thing that makes its food from sunlight and has just one type of complex cell.

CLASS
A scientific group that includes animals with the same body plan, such as birds or bony fish.

COLONY
A group of animals living together.

CRITICALLY ENDANGERED
Describes a species that is at extremely high risk of very soon becoming extinct.

CRUSTACEAN
An arthropod with two pairs of antennae on its head, such as a crab.

CURRENT
A stream of water that flows through the ocean.

CYANOBACTERIA
Bacteria that make their own food from sunlight.

DIATOM
A microscopic chromist with a single cell.

DORSAL FIN
A fin on the back of a fish or a cetacean.

EIDERDOWN
A quilt made with the soft inner feathers of a duck or other bird.

ENDANGERED
Describes a species that is likely to become extinct in the near future.

EVOLVE
To change gradually over time.

EXOSKELETON
The hard outer covering of some invertebrates.

FILTER FEEDING
Straining food from the water using comb- or net-like body parts.

FIN
A body part that juts from the body of fish and some other water-living animals, helping them swim.

FISH
A water-living animal that takes oxygen from the water using gills and usually has fins.

FRESHWATER
Unsalted water, such as rivers, lakes, and ponds.

GENUS
A scientific group that includes species very similar to each other.

GILL
An organ in fish that takes oxygen from water.

GLAND
A body part that makes a substance for use in the body or for release.

GLOBAL WARMING
Rising world temperatures caused mainly by human activities.